HAYES PRESS

More Than a Saviour

Exploring the Person & Work of Christ

First edition

This book was professionally typeset on Reedsy.
Find out more at reedsy.com

Contents

1

THE RADIANCE OF GOD'S GLORY (DAVID WOODS)

"He is the radiance of the glory of God" (Heb.1:3).

On a recent holiday I enjoyed the pleasure of an early morning jog. As the country roads turned towards the east, the low position of the sun in the winter sky made it difficult to see anything else in front of me. The brightness of the sun on that clear morning was blinding, and care was needed to ensure I didn't run into oncoming traffic or some obstacles that could trip me up. It was glorious, yet, at the same time, a little uncomfortable!

On a Galilee mountain the disciples Peter, James and John had an experience that was even more glorious. Shortly before they climbed that mountain to pray with Jesus, Peter had declared that he and the other disciples were convinced that Jesus was the Christ, the promised Messiah and the Son of the Living God (1). There, on that mountaintop, it was as if God wanted to confirm that fact unmistakably, and Jesus' face and form was changed in a unique way. Matthew tells us, "he was transfigured before them, and his face shone like the sun, and his clothes became white as light" (2). Jesus Christ shone brighter than the sun! Something of His heavenly glory, that was His from all eternity (3), burst through and astounded those men. In Hebrews 1:3 we're told that "He is the radiance of the glory of God." Forever, God's Son has been radiating and shining forth as the glory of God.

David could write in Psalm 19:1, "The heavens declare the glory of God." He was awestruck as he viewed, without the aid of modern telescopes, the grandeur of God's creation and the stars that filled the night sky. For him they declared the glory of God. And the vast universe that we can peer into today still does the same! But the heavens are not the glory of God; they are only a declaration of God's glory, which is far and above anything that He has created. God's glory is His alone! It's useful to try to define 'glory'. A suggested definition is: 'God's glory is the beauty of His manifold perfections. It can refer to the bright and awesome radiance that sometimes breaks forth in visible manifestations. Or it can refer to the infinite moral excellence of His character. In either case it signifies a reality of infinite greatness and worth' (4).

In Hebrews 1:3 the Greek word ('doxa') that's translated 'glory' has the sense of 'something, or someone that owns a high estimation or opinion, and therefore has honour that results from that good opinion' (5). Realising that the glory of God we are considering in this scripture is the 'infinite excellence of His character', we come to appreciate that God the Son is the radiance of the unparalleled and unmatched being, person and character of God.

This brings us, for a moment, into the mind-bending truth of the Godhead: God who is one, yet three distinct persons – God the Father, God the Son and God the Holy Spirit – who are entirely and completely

God in themselves! Jesus said that, "God is spirit ..." (6) and John declared that "no one has ever seen God; the only God, who is at the Father's side, he has made him known" (7). So, we're right to think that it's God the Father being referred to, "whom no one has ever seen or can see" (8). Yet, by the grace of God, we're able to see and know God, and His glory, through the person of God the Son, and the working of God the Holy Spirit, who indwells all believers (9). We are helped by God Himself to understand something of the true magnitude of what we're considering here: that being fully God, God the Son radiates everything that God is in His infinite being and person.

Radiance means a 'shining forth', or the 'light that shines from a luminous body' (10). Just like the bright sun radiates a blinding light by virtue of what it is, so God the Son radiates the awesome glory of God by virtue of who He is. And He has done so for all eternity, and will continue to do so for all eternity!

Isaiah and Ezekiel had awesome visions of heaven, and they both saw one like a man on the throne in heaven. It was a glorious sight that was almost beyond description (11), but they were looking at Him who is the radiance of God's glory, the eternal Son of God. And this was prior to His "being born in the likeness of men ... being found in human form" (12). Now we stand in awe of the grand plans of God, that He would reveal Himself and His glory to us, through God the eternal Son, by His taking on human flesh.

God had declared something of His glory in the creation of the universe. He had declared something of His glory through the giving of the Law and the Word of God that today comprises our Old Testaments. But that wasn't enough. God the Son, the one who is the radiance of the glory of God, walked on this earth with us. "And the Word became flesh and dwelt among us, and we have seen his glory, glory as of the only Son from the Father, full of grace and truth" (13) This was the full expression of God's glory to us.

In everything He was excellent. He was infinitely better than any who had lived before, and any of His contemporaries. He is superior in all ways to any who have lived since. He was sinless perfection (14), and He exuded the character of God in all that He did, while subjecting and humbling Himself to the limitations of human experience. Peter, recounting his experience on that mountaintop, wrote that "he received honour and glory from God the Father, and the voice was borne to him by the Majestic Glory, 'This is my beloved Son, with whom I am well pleased,' we ourselves heard this very voice borne from heaven, for we were with him on the holy mountain" (15). God declared from heaven on three occasions His delight in God the Son, the one who became the Son of Man, who was the radiance of the glory of God in every aspect of His life.

John wrote that the Lord's first miracle, changing water into wine at the wedding party in Cana, "manifested his glory" (16). Through the wonder of His countless miracles, the glory of God was also seen. He is the radiance of the glory of God. There is none that compares to Him, and to what He has done. But there was more that the Lord Jesus wanted His disciples to know about the eternal glory of God. He prayed the night before Calvary, "Father, I desire that they also, whom you have given me, may be with me where I am, to see my glory [doxa] that you have given me because you loved me before the foundation of the world" (17). For all eternity, those who are His will delight in Him who will forever be the radiance of the glory of God. It's through the person of our Lord Jesus Christ that we will be eternally introduced to the beauty of God's manifold perfections.

It required the eternal Son to humble Himself "by becoming obedient to the point of death, even death on a cross" (18), so that we sinners, who had fallen so far short of recognising and acknowledging God's glory (19), might be brought into the "light of the knowledge of the glory of God in the face of Jesus Christ" (20). Later in Hebrews we're encouraged to run, "looking to Jesus, the founder and perfecter of our faith, who for the joy that was set before him endured the cross, despising the shame, and is seated at the right hand of the throne of God" (21). Running and looking to Him who is the radiance of the glory of God, should be a glorious experience. Dark shadows are cast on us when something comes between the Son and us. What things are casting shadows in our lives and block our view of the glory of God as we see it in the face of Jesus? Remove them!

In the clear, unobstructed light of His infinite perfections and eternal excellence, things that are of fleeting and fading value must be put in their proper place. There is nothing and no one to compare to our God, and the one who is the radiance of His glory. Enjoy Him now, and forever.

References: (1) Matt.16:16 (2) Matt.17:2 (3) Jn.17:5 (4) J. Piper, Desiring God: Meditations of a Christian Hedonist, 2004 (5) W.E. Vine, Vine's Expository Dictionary of Old & New Testament Words: Glory, Glorious (6) Jn.4:24 (7) Jn.1:18 (8) 1 Tim.6:16 (9) Rom.8:9,11 (10) W.E. Vine, Vine's Expository Dictionary of Old & New Testament Words: Bright, Brightness (11) see Is.6 and Ezek.1 (12) Phil.2:7-8 (13) Jn.1:14 (14) 1 Jn.3:5 (15) 2 Pet.1:17-18 (16) Jn.2:11 (17) Jn.17:24 (18) Phil.2:8 (19) Rom.3:23 (20) 2 Cor.4:6 (21) Heb.12:2

Bible quotations from the ESV.

2

THE EXACT IMPRINT OF GOD'S NATURE (KARL SMITH)

"He is ... the exact imprint of his nature..."

In the last chapter, we saw how the description of the Lord Jesus in Hebrews 1:3 as "the radiance of the glory of God." It focuses on how the Lord Jesus shines out one particular aspect of God: His 'glory'. Now we move on to how the Lord Jesus expresses all of God's innermost being: His 'nature'. "He is ... the exact imprint of his nature", the writer to the Hebrews continues in the English Standard Version. The Revised version chooses the word 'substance' instead of 'nature'. The Greek word both are trying to translate is 'hypostasis'. This was a word that had been used four hundred years or so beforehand by Plato and other Greek philosophers to mean the real nature of something, underlying its appearance.

Readers familiar with C.S. Lewis's Narnia series will remember the description of heaven that appears at the end of the final book in the series, 'The Last Battle.' In his fictitious universe, Lewis imagines

6

heaven to be a larger and perfected version of the places they have loved throughout their lives. Perhaps fancifully, the book explains that the England the characters had lived in before their death and the Narnia known by those who had lived there were merely shadow lands, which give physical expression to the real England and the real Narnia that exist as part of the real world above. 'The reason why we loved the old Narnia is that it sometimes looks a little like this', a unicorn rapturously explains to the children. Their friend the Professor replies, "It's all in Plato, all in Plato: bless me, what do they teach them at these schools!"

Plato, in his 'Republic', compared the world to a cave whose inhabitants see only distorted shadows, thrown on the roof by a crackling fire, of what is really there in the larger world outside. The external material things we can see are bound to be illusionary in some way in Plato's thought, just like the shadows in the cave. Underlying each one, however, is an inner nature, its substance, its reality. One of the words Plato uses for this is its 'hypostasis', the same word translated 'nature' or 'substance' in Hebrews 1:3.

The nature or substance of something, then, is no woolly theory about it, but something solid you could rely on if only you could grasp it. The word literally means 'underneath standing' and this signals how foundational it is. In fact, by the time of the New Testament, the Greek word had come to mean an absolute confidence in the thing under discussion and it is used in this way later on in Hebrews - e.g. "Now faith is the assurance [this time the King James Version does translate this word as 'substance'] of things hoped for" (1). But how can we with our tiny finite minds ever hope to grasp the nature of God firmly enough to have this kind of confidence in Him?

He wanted to make His invisible nature visible to us. He sent us more than a flickering shadow. In fact, He sent His Son who is "the exact imprint of his nature". The New International Version translates this word as "the exact representation of His being". Other scriptures such as 2 Corinthians 4:4 and Colossians 1:15 talk about the Lord Jesus as "the image of God" and "the image of the invisible God". In these verses the Holy Spirit chooses the word 'eikon', which we still use in English as 'icon'. This emphasises the visual element of what is seen, something you can look at. Hebrews 1:3 uses a deeper word, which is found only once in our Bibles, 'charakter'. This word, by contrast, emphasises the process by which the image is made. It was a symbol created by an engraving tool on something like a coin; or perhaps a seal on a ring was pressed in hot wax. When it cooled down, the image left in it would show exactly what was on the seal. We still use this word in a similar way. In printing, a character such as a letter or number on the page reflects exactly what is on the head of the typewriter or on the printing press. To take yet another example, by looking at the imprint in the snow, you can see exactly the pattern of the boot that has walked in it.

The Lord Jesus is not a rough approximation, a vague idea of what God is like. He is not a shadow of God's nature, as in Plato's cave. Shadows lengthen out at twilight and shrink in towards mid-day. They dance and move in bizarre ways as the fire crackles. He is not someone from whom we can piece together a good guess as to God's nature. The unfathomable nature of God is represented exactly in His Son, 'the exact imprint of his nature'. This happens to an extent in human families. We carry genetic information in our DNA that often causes us to resemble our parents, whether in looks or character. How often have you heard someone say, "So-and-so is the image of his father"? No-one looks precisely identical to his father, however. We all have features of our own to add to the mix. The Lord Jesus is the express image of His Father's substance with nothing added into the mix from elsewhere.

Of all the 'many ways' God had spoken through the prophets mentioned in Hebrews 1, none had been so precise an expression of His being as this expression "in these last days" when "he has spoken to us by his Son" (2). This, however, is not to downplay the Old Testament Scriptures. They form part of the divine Word of God as the main means by which we learn about who God is today. As our inner thoughts need words to communicate them to others, so the Bible communicates the truth of God to us perfectly and directly. Because of the limitations of our human languages and our finite minds, however, God sent His Son to communicate, not only His truth, but His whole nature. Many of those who saw Him would not be able to read the Scriptures, although they could hear them read aloud. Nevertheless, the Lord Jesus was a walking, talking Bible to them in His actions and personality as much as in His teaching. It is no accident that the Lord Jesus is also called 'The Word' (3).

Looking at the Lord Jesus is precisely equivalent to looking at God. That's why He could tell Philip, "Whoever has seen me has seen the Father" (4). I suspect that the angels in heaven cannot directly see or even understand the nature of God, but perhaps even there He delights in revealing it through His Son. Certainly, however, God was seen through His Son on earth. Those who saw Him act saw the way God acts: "the Son can do nothing of his own accord, but only what he sees the Father doing. For whatever the Father does, that the Son does likewise" (5). He gave the example of raising the dead, something only God could do (6). Soon Jairus's daughter and Lazarus would be able to testify that the Son was the image of the Father in this respect, making God's power to raise the dead spectacularly visible.

We look forward to the day when He will raise our loved ones who have died in Christ – and then ourselves – to enjoy eternal life in new bodies.

Equally they could be confident that the teaching they heard from Him was not different by a single syllable from what God Himself wanted to teach them: "I do nothing on my own authority, but speak just as the Father taught me" (7).

Some aspects of God's nature as expressed in Christ shocked enemy and disciple alike, such as the profound holiness that extended beyond external things into the hidden motives – and also the consuming desire to extend forgiveness to even the most unpalatable of people. "Who can forgive sins but God alone?" asked the scribes, not realising that God's exact imprint was among them (8). Their concept of God's nature was too small. Human philosophy cannot comprehend its fullness in words and concepts, so God sent His Son for us to see it expressed in a person, "For in him the whole fullness of deity dwells bodily" (9).

References: (1) Heb.11:1 (2) Heb.1:1-2 (3) Jn.1:1-14 (4) Jn.14:9 (5) Jn.5:19 (6) Jn.5:21 (7) Jn.8:28 (8) Mk.2:7 (9) Col.2:9

Bible quotations from the ESV.

3

THE UPHOLDER OF ALL THINGS (STEPHEN HICKLING)

"By faith we understand that the worlds were prepared by the word of God ..." (1).

This takes us right back to the beginning, to Genesis 1. It was by the mouth of God that the universe was created and we know that the creation was effected through the Son. Whilst Hebrews 11:3 has the command of God in creative power in view, however, Hebrews 1:3 focuses on the Son's word of sustaining power: "The Son ... sustaining all things by his powerful word" (2). 'Sustaining' conveys the dual thought of support and movement. By His every word, God the Son not only upholds the universe, but regulates it and carries it forward. His powerful imperative is the reason the universe both exists as it does and continues to exist.

"For by [or in] Him all things were created, both in the heavens and on earth, visible and invisible, whether thrones or dominions or rulers or authorities — all things have been created through Him and for Him.

He is before all things, and in Him all things hold together" (3). In Colossians 1, the Lord's priority and authority, vis-à-vis His creation, are clear: all things were created by Him and for Him. More than that, though, all things were created in Him. That seems to express something of the dependence which the creation has on the Lord. It is solely on account of all things being the result of His creative design, will and continued supply of energy that our universe hangs together as it does. Don't the laws of nature bear out so clearly the harmony and solidarity of the Godhead and testify also to the Son's tireless work of upholding?

And yet, what a marked contrast we see in the 'upholder of all things', as He was led away to be crucified. We read of Him: "Then they brought Him to the place Golgotha, which is translated, Place of a Skull" (4). The same word, which is used of His upholding power in Hebrews 1:3, is here used of the men who 'brought' Him to Golgotha. Of course, they had no knowledge of the sustaining power of the One they bore. They saw a man exhausted from trial and false testimony, battered by the scourging of Roman soldiers, and agonising at what He alone knew lay before Him; and so they carried Him to the Place of the Skull. We rejoice at the grace of God in allowing the 'upholder of all things' to be brought by sinful men to Calvary!

Yet, physically weakened though the Saviour was (struggling even to 'uphold' His own cross – see Luke 23:26), how thankful we are that "He himself bore our sins in his body on the tree, so that we might die to sins and live for righteousness" (5). He carried a weight far greater at Calvary than the cross of wood he carried to Calvary. In God's mercy, we will never know how heavy that cup of God's wrath against sin was; He bore it on the cross, where He drained it completely, even to the very dregs.

By His Powerful Word

The Lord Jesus is the Word (Greek: 'logos') that was with God, that was God and that became flesh (6). 'Logos' means the expression of thought and, as the Word, Christ is the full expression of the heart and mind of God. In His person, character and actions, He fully communicates to us all that we are able to comprehend about God. In Hebrews 1:3, though, the focus is on the detail of His every utterance (Greek: 'Rhema'). The words He speaks are full of power to sustain; they uphold the universe!

The power of divine utterance was evident in creation. God spoke and it was so and He saw that it was good. Just so, the words of the Lord Jesus carry dynamic force. After all, He told His disciples that He did not speak on His own, but spoke only what He was commanded to speak by His Father. Even the words He used were the ones His Father gave Him to speak and time after time in the gospel narratives we see their wonderful power.

The Jews often expressed the power of God in their writings by phrases such as "He carries all His creatures" or "He bears His world". The writer to the Hebrews was giving clear testimony to the deity of the Lord Jesus, then, in stating that by His powerful words, the Lord sustains all things. What a striking contrast there is between the power of man and the power of God: man demonstrates his power by acts of great exertion, by force and by violence; yet it is characteristic of God alone that He need only speak to work wonders.

For Nothing Will Be Impossible With God (7)

Literally, this verse tells us that no word (Greek: rhema) of God shall be without power. The Lord never wastes a word. Everything He says is vitally important and never fails to accomplish the purposes for which it is spoken. As disciples of the Lord Jesus, we would do well to hang on His every word, for not one of them will return to Him void. Of course, the whole Bible is the inspired Word of God, but many of us will have Bibles which emphasise the spoken words of the Lord Jesus in some way (perhaps highlighting them with the use of red text). Time spent in the gospels, studying the records of the Lord Jesus' sayings will be time well-spent.

Ephesians 6 contains the passage of Scripture which talks about the Christian's armour: those things with which we should clothe ourselves daily if we are to withstand the attacks of the evil one. "And take the helmet of salvation, and the sword of the Spirit, which is the word of God" (8). 'Word' here is 'rhema' – we need a firm grip on the individual words or sayings of God if we're to succeed in our spiritual warfare. For those of us in the west, the Word of God is freely available. Many of us will carry the whole Bible in our pockets on our PDAs and smartphones; the words of the Lord are at our fingertips. There is, however, still great benefit to be had in memorising these words. How much better-equipped for battle will we be with small phrases and verses committed to memory! We need only recall the Lord's temptation in the wilderness to answer that question. God desires that we learn His words and He will enable us, by His Spirit, to do so if we patiently dedicate time to this exercise.

Our Lord Jesus Christ is the sustainer of all things: all things live, breathe and have their being in Him. How much more inclined is He to bear up those He calls His own! Shouldn't the security of the everlasting arms evoke a desire in us to pay close attention to His words? His are the words of abundant life; if they abide in us, those words will empower us to live in the freedom for which we were saved, rather than as slaves again to things from which He died to set us free.

References: (1) Heb.11:3 (2) Heb.1:3 NIV (3) Col.1:16–17 (4) Mk.15:22 (5) 1 Pet.2:24 NIV (6) Jn.1:1,14 (7) Lk.1:37 (8) Eph.6:17

Bible quotations from the NASB, unless otherwise stated.

4

THE SUPREME HEAD OF THE BODY (JAMES NEEDHAM)

It was a wonderful day in the history of Israel! Responding to David's rallying cry, and the devotion with which he had given his own treasure for the construction of a house for God, the leaders of the people stepped forward and with their whole heart gave freely to the Lord. Uplifted by the selflessness of the people, David blessed God, from whose hand they had first received it all:

"Yours, O LORD, is the greatness and the power and the glory and the victory and the majesty, for all that is in the heavens and in the earth is yours. Yours is the kingdom, O LORD, and von are exalted as head above all" (1).

Headship has to do with authority and direction. As the head is above the human body, directing the members according to the exercise of the mind, so the head of any organisation is its controlling power; the one with the prominent place of rule, giving direction according to his will. As Head above all, the God of heaven has no equal, for, "The LORD has established his throne in the heavens, and his kingdom rules over all"

16

(2).

It was a lesson Nebuchadnezzar had to learn. Restored from his humiliation, having dwelt with the beasts of the field, the king of Babylon praised God Most High: "for his dominion is an everlasting dominion ... he does according to his will among the host of heaven and among the inhabitants of the earth" (3). And so He does, for He is head above all!

Christ as Head Above All

Later in his prophecy (4), Daniel was caused to see the Ancient of Days take His seat, enthroned among the multitudes which serve Him. One like a son of man came and stood before the throne to receive from God an everlasting dominion and a kingdom that shall not be destroyed. We are left in no doubt who received this dominion from the Head above all, since it is confirmed by the words of the Lord Jesus Himself: "all authority in heaven and on earth has been given to me" (5). It was this authority that occupied His mind even in the pain of the night of His betrayal, for as He rose from supper to wash His disciples' feet, He did so in the knowledge that the Father had given all things into his hands (6).

The power, the glory, the victory and the majesty which David identified in God as Head above all were perfected in the glorious triumph of Christ. He is the great victor over death and hell, and God has seated Him at His right hand far above all rule and authority and power and dominion ... he put all things under his feet (7). It has been the response of God to the work of Calvary to glorify His Son to an unparalleled position, inviting Him to "Sit at my right hand" (8). As Peter declared on the day of Pentecost, God has made His enemies a footstool for His feet, and "made him both Lord and Christ, this Jesus whom you crucified" (9).

The lowly man of Calvary has been highly exalted; from the depths of His humiliation, He has been made Head above all! (10).

Head of the Church - His Supremacy

It is in this context of His supremacy that we are first introduced to the Lord Jesus as Head over the Church, which is His body. Though concealed in the Old Testament scriptures, the building of this Church has been one of the great, eternal purposes of God. It consists of all those who, beginning on the day of Pentecost until the Lord returns for His own, have been baptised by the Lord Himself in the Spirit at the point of personal salvation (11). In his letter to the Ephesians, Paul described this Church in exalted terms. It is the mystery of Christ, once hidden from generations, but now revealed through the apostles and prophets by the Holy Spirit. This mystery, Paul said, is that the Gentiles are fellow heirs, members of the same body, and partakers of the promise in Christ Jesus through the gospel (12).

To Paul was given this message of the unsearchable riches of Christ, that he might, through his ministry, unveil the plan of the mystery ... "so that through the church the manifold wisdom of God might now be made known to the rulers and authorities in the heavenly places" (13). Once hidden in the heart of God. this church is now the revelation of God's manifold wisdom, His open proclamation of victory to the spiritual powers arrayed against Him. It is the assertion of the efficacy of His grace in Christ, and the manifestation of the irreversible triumph of His work.

Who then possesses sufficient value to be head over this glorious body? Only Christ! So, to the Church God gave His Son, whom first He had made head over all things, so that the one who fills all in all might bring divine purpose to completion, resulting in the Body reflecting nothing but Christ Himself (14). This connection between the supremacy of Christ and His headship over the Body is renewed in Colossians 1. There we read of His eternal deity, and of His role as creator. And there we read, in the middle of this declaration of His pre-eminence, that he is the head of the body, the church (15). Exalted high as Head of the body, the Lord Jesus directs this perfected company of saints who have been called, justified and glorified by His own atoning work. Here is the manifold wisdom of God laid bare to both the seen and unseen realms! Here is His triumph revealed; the exaltation of His Son declared in an office which proclaims His glory!

Head of the Church - His Intimacy

The theme of Ephesians 1 is developed in later chapters. In chapter 4, the relationship of the Head to the body is seen in the unity of a single organism (16). From the Head, the whole body is joined together, every joint and every limb supplied with its purpose and direction, that the body might grow and build itself up in love. Love remains the theme in chapter 5, where Paul uses the figure of marriage to describe the intimacy between the Head and the body. Christ's love for His Church was wonderfully shown when He gave Himself up for her, that by the shedding of His blood He might make her a glorious thing –sanctified, cleansed, holy and faultless. And as Head of the Church. He is not detached, ruling over her from a distance. Rather. He remains her loving preserver: intimately connected to care for her, nourishing and cherishing her as a faithful husband his wife.

This work of nourishing was seen in His ascension. From far above all the heavens, He allocated the gifts of the Spirit among the Church, that from His hand the saints might be equipped for the work of ministry, for building up the body of Christ (17). The purpose is high indeed, for the gifts which He has so liberally bestowed are intended for the nourishment of the church He preserves, that we. His members, might be equipped to attain the unity of the faith and the knowledge of Him - that, growing under His watchful, loving care, we might attain to the measure of the stature of the fullness of Christ (18).

Holding Fast the Head

To the Church, God has given a head who is supreme above all. It is a measure both of the greatness of Christ and the preciousness of the Church that He who fills all in all should be made Head of such a body. Yet, with that great privilege comes the challenge to His own. Until the day when He calls us to meet with Him in the clouds, it is our responsibility, our joy, to grow up in every way into him who is the head, into Christ (19). And that requires that in our daily lives we hold fast to the Head (20) since it is only through active communion with Him that those within His body shall receive the sustenance required to grow within this glorious body which proclaims God's wisdom throughout the heavens and the earth. The one who became our Saviour at Calvary has promised He will never let us go (21). In response, it must be our unceasing purpose to hold fast to Him as Head of the Body, and so proclaim His love and glory in our generation.

References: (1) 1 Chron. 29:11 (2) Ps.103:19 (3) Dan.4:34-35 (4) Dan.7:9-14 (5) Matt.28:18 (6) Jn.13:3 (7) Eph.1:21-22 (8) Ps.110:1; Heb.1:13 (9) Acts 2:34-36 (10) Col.2:10 (11) 1 Cor.12:13 (12) Eph.3:4-6 (13) Eph.3:8-10 (14) Eph.1:22-23 (15) Col.1:15-20 (16) Eph.4:15-16 (17) Eph.4:12 (18) Eph.4:13 (19) Eph.4:15 (20) Col.2:19 (21) Jn 10:28

Bible quotations from the ESV.

5

THE STONE, THE HEAD OF THE CORNER (JOHN DRAIN)

In the Scriptures we may trace many relationships in which Christ stands to created beings. Each of these relationships has its own particular significance in the general presentation of the excellencies of our Lord Jesus Christ. His headship, emphasizing as it does truths relating to His supremacy, demands careful consideration. Headship speaks of exaltation and authority. The head is one to whom others are subordinate. Functions of the head may be seen in controlling, in co-ordinating, in cohering. One has said that in headship we have that which combines "exaltation with the vital union necessary to organism". As we examine the Scriptures we find in various contexts relevant emphasis on these meanings of headship. In the last chapter we considered Christ as the Head of the Body. And now we come to two other elements of the Headship of Christ.

In Matthew 21 there is brought before us a significant stage in the public ministry of the Lord Jesus. After riding into Jerusalem on an ass, in fulfilment of what was spoken by the prophet Zechariah, the Lord entered the Temple and taught and acted with such authority that a crisis in His relations with the leaders of the Israel nation was inevitable. Two important parables were spoken by Christ at that time. In the second one He told about a householder who planted a vineyard. After much disappointment because of the attitude of the husbandmen towards his servants, the householder finally decided to send his son. He said, "They will reverence my son." But the son, too, was rejected and was killed.

With great skill the Lord was drawing for those leaders of the people an unmistakable picture of how the purposes of God had been resisted by the Israel people. In the crisis of those purposes God sent His Son into the world. The Head of all principality left heaven and came to this speck in the universe, to this abode of the human race. He was seen a Babe, a Youth, a Man. He is the great Mystery of God. But He came to earth to be rejected. Addressing the chief priests and the Pharisees, the Lord Jesus said, "Did ye never read in the Scriptures, *"The Stone which the builders rejected, the same was made the Head of the corner: This was from the Lord, and it is marvellous in our eyes?"* (Matt.21:42).

This quotation from Psalm 118 shows very clearly that the One whom the leaders of the Israel nation refused and rejected has been received back by God to occupy in heaven the place of authority as the Head of the corner. This Stone was to become the Keystone in God's dealings with men and women. The Lord said, *"He that falleth on this Stone shall be broken to pieces: but on whomsoever it shall fall, it will scatter him as dust."*

After Christ had been raised from the dead and had returned to heaven His servants, by His command and authority, witnessed for Him in Jerusalem. This led to the arrest of Peter and John and to their appearance before the leaders of the Israel nation for examination. It is worthy of notice that those same men who listened to the parable and to its application, as recorded in Matthew 21 heard once more, this time from the Spirit-filled servant of the Lord, those searching words, *"He is the Stone which was set at nought of you the builders, which was made the Head of the corner."*

And Peter added, *"And in none other is there salvation: for neither is there any other name under heaven, that is given among men, wherein we must be saved"* (Acts 4:11,12). Thus the revelation of God directs us to a very important aspect of the Headship of Christ. He is the Head of the corner in heaven. Before He left His disciples to return to take His place at His Father's right hand the Lord said, *"All authority hath been given unto Me in heaven and on earth"* (Matt.28:18). This authority may manifest itself in blessing or in judgement.

In his first epistle Peter deals with the purpose of God in having a house on earth. He shows that in that purpose it is the will of God that believers in Christ, those who have known what it is to be saved, to be redeemed, to be born again, as referred to in chapter 1, should be brought into a relationship with Himself through Christ the living Stone by reason of which as living stones they are built up to be a spiritual house. Pursuing his exposition, Peter says, *"Because it is contained in Scripture, Behold, I lay in Zion a chief corner Stone, elect, precious: and he that believeth on Him shall not be put to shame. For you therefore which believe is the preciousness: but for such as disbelieve, The Stone which the builders rejected, the same was made the Head of the Corner; and, A Stone of stumbling, and a Rock of offence; for they stumble at the word, being disobedient: whereunto also they were appointed"* (1 Pet.2:6-8).

We can observe in these two quotations blessing and judgement. Blessing comes to those who believe. Judgement comes to those who disbelieve. Israel stumbled at the Stone of stumbling because they were unbelieving and disobedient. They were not appointed to be disobedient but as disobedient ones they were appointed to stumble. It is important to notice the words, *"Behold I lay in Zion a chief corner Stone, elect, precious."* This is what God the Father did to His Son who was rejected on earth. He made Him the Head of the Corner; He is the chief corner Stone. God intends that what He has done in heaven should have practical consequences on earth. To the Son all authority has been given in heaven, and it is God's purpose that this should be acknowledged on earth. Things will be right in so far as they are right with Him who is the Head and the chief corner Stone. When Paul wrote to the Corinthians he referred to the church of God in Corinth as being God's building. Then, commenting on his own activities in relation to the establishment of this building, he said, *"As a wise master-builder I laid a foundation."* A building needs a foundation.

Let it be emphasized that Paul did not lay a foundation of his own production. He wrote, *"Other foundation can no man lay than that which is laid, which is Jesus Christ."* What Paul did in Corinth was to give to Christ in his preaching and teaching the place that God had given to Him in heaven. This same important truth is found in what Paul said concerning others, *"Being built upon the foundation of the apostles and prophets, Christ Jesus Himself being the chief corner Stone"* (Eph.2:20). The precious Saviour of sinners is the Lord of the universe, the One in whom divine authority is vested and through whom it is exercised. It is very important that those who know that Christ is their Saviour should know and acknowledge His Lordship.

When writing concerning the resurrection and exaltation of Christ, Paul said, *"He* [God the Father] *put all things in subjection under His feet, and gave Him to be Head over all things to the Church, which is His Body, the fulness of Him that filleth all in all"* (Eph.1:22,23). When God was about to make the first man, Adam, God said, *"Let us make man in our image, after our likeness: and let them have dominion over the fish of the sea, and over the fowl of the air, and over the cattle, and over all the earth, and over every creeping thing that creepeth upon the earth"* (Gen.1:26). And so *"the LORD God formed man of the dust of the ground, and breathed into his nostrils the breath of life; and man became a living soul"* (Gen.2:7). Adam became God's overlord on earth, all things were put under his feet.

Though he held such an exalted place in divine purpose, Adam was not complete according to the mind of God. *"The Lord God said, 'It is not good that the man should be alone: I will make him an help meet for him.'"* From the man the LORD God took a rib which He made a woman and brought her to the man. Hence, while it is true that in Eden's garden there were two distinct and separable personalities, Adam and Eve, it is also true that in woman man found his complement. By divine appointment, Adam was head over all things, and it was to one in a position so important as this that Eve was joined, not only to share his glory and honour but also to be his fulness.

In the revelation of God concerning the Lord Jesus Christ we find precious truth which far transcends anything which we may discern in the instructive story of Adam. Adam's authority was defined and restricted, as we have noticed in Genesis 1. But in the blessed Lord Jesus we see One who sits at the right hand of the Father, *"far above all rule, and authority, and power, and dominion, and every name that is named, not only in this world but also in that which is to come"* (Eph.1:21). Under His feet all created things, without reserve or restriction, have been put in subjection. It is in this high position and relationship as Head over all things that He has been given to the Church, which is His Body. The Church will share His glory and honour. The Body is the fulness of Him that filleth all things in all.

The One who is Head of the vast angelic creation, who is the Head of the corner in the heavenly arrangement of things, who is the Head over all things to the Church which is His Body is also *"the Head of the Church"* (Eph.5:22), *"the Head of the Body"* (Col.1:18).

6

THE CHRIST, THE SON MESSIAH (KEITH DORRICOTT)

For most of this world's history, Christ the Son of God has been invisible to mankind. Even when, almost two thousand years ago, He came into this world as 'Jesus' for a short while, He was in effect in disguise; His supreme visible glory was hidden (1). Most people developed wrong notions about who He was, despite the unique evidence of what He did, as Isaiah the prophet had written about long before (2). This evidence was confirmed to John the Baptist, who was looking for Him at the time (3). And so there were relatively few who were able to see Him then as the one who was clearly superior to all others.

But one day in the future He will come back here in His visible majestic glory – which He now possesses as a glorified man in heaven. Every eye will see Him at that time (4) and know exactly who He is. Every knee will bow down and honour Him for who He is (5). And everyone's tongue will confess the fact that He is indeed Lord of all (6). There will be no exceptions. For He is the one and only Messiah (the 'Christ') promised by God from long ago (7) – the one uniquely chosen and anointed by God and consecrated by Him to be king and priest. Although He has already been given all authority in heaven and on earth (8). He does not yet exercise it over those people who are not willingly subject to Him; instead, He holds it back – but only for a time. All who are opposed to Him will most certainly be put under His complete rule by His Father (9); after He will yet come to earth in full glory. Of this there is no doubt.

His Qualification

Why Christ? Why does He get this supreme honour? The reason is that He has clearly demonstrated that He is, by far, the most qualified for it – in fact the only one. The epistle to the Hebrews makes His qualification very clear, and describes Him categorically as being superior to all others. It shows, for example, that He is greater than Moses, who was exemplary as a faithful servant in the house of God on earth, the tabernacle constructed in the wilderness; however it was only temporary, and just a reflection of the true one (10). Christ is forever Son over God's true house.

It shows how He is superior to Joshua as a leader, who took the people of Israel into their Promised Land after Moses, but was not able to bring them all the way to Mount Zion, God's chosen place for His people to worship Him then (11). Christ has brought us into God with no barrier or distance left (12). And it shows that He is superior to Aaron, Israel's first high priest (13) who established the priestly order of Aaron for others to follow under the old covenant. However, the law of that covenant could never bring people all the way to God; there was always a barrier because of sin – which Christ removed by the sacrifice of Himself (14). And, more than that, the Hebrews' epistle begins by showing how He is also vastly superior to the highest rank and capability of created beings: angels.

There are immense multitudes of angelic beings (15), they have great power which they use in God's service, and some of them serve in the very presence of God (16). They are His messengers and agents, but they are limited in how they can carry this out. But the Son has no such limitations. As Jesus Himself said: *"... no one knows the Son except the Father, and no one knows the Father except the Son and anyone to whom the Son chooses to reveal him"* (17).

When He came initially in the flesh, He was willingly subjected for a while to a lower place than angels occupy (18), to become a man in order to redeem men to God. But no more. They will come into this world in a great future display of glory, but they will come to accompany Him.

From the Psalms

The first chapter of Hebrews quotes several Psalms, where the glory of the Son, in contrast with that of created angelic beings, is expressed by God, well in advance of His coming. God cannot forsake His Word (19), and so each of these has been destined to come true with complete certainty.

The chapter begins by declaring the fact that not one of them has ever been called "My Son" by God the Father. The Son of God is indeed God Himself, part of the very Godhead. His Father made this clear when He addressed Him personally as God: *"... to the Son He says, 'Your throne, O God, is forever and ever'"* (20). He has now been established clearly by God as the heir of all things and all will be subject to Him (21). Even the angels are to worship Him (22). This is something totally reserved for the Godhead, as the apostle John found out when he was about to bow down to the angel who was showing him marvellous things to come; he was told, *"Do not do that ... Worship God"* (23). Anything else is idolatry.

The Son will have total authority over all the nations. He will indeed be the King of all other kings (24). His throne will never come to an end – He will never be replaced. His rule will be fully just and equitable (25) because He Himself has demonstrated that He loves what is right and hates what is wrong (26). There will be no compromise; never any devious intentions or ulterior motives from Him as world ruler (27), for the first time in human history.

"My Son"

The relationship between the Father and the Son has always been unique. Jesus said to His Father on the way to Calvary: *"You loved Me before the foundation of the world"* (28). This is far beyond God's relationship with any angel. He never called any of them *"My Son"*, or said to them, *"I will be to him a father, and he shall be to me a son"* (29). *"My Son"* is a term of great endearment and of total satisfaction to God His Father. During Christ's time on earth, twice God called out audibly from heaven with the words, *"This is my beloved Son, in whom I am well pleased."* It happened at His baptism, as He was committing Himself to fulfil all righteousness in the service He was about to begin (30), and again as He was committing Himself to go to Jerusalem to complete that work (31). And when the work of Calvary was over, God raised Him from the dead, never to die again, and so demonstrated by divine power that He was indeed the Son of God (32). The unique deity of Christ is beyond question.

God was then able to fully exalt Him to His own right hand, the place of all honour and authority, and make Him the supreme King-Priest forever. This is His inheritance. What delight that must have given God as His Father, as He anointed Him (not any others) with *"the oil of gladness more than Your companions"* (33). The words describing God as the everlasting creator (34) are applied to the Son of God in this Hebrews epistle (35), for He is the one through whom everything was created.

His rule shall never end and He will outlast everything He made. He has been given total authority over everything that exists (36), His Father will subdue all opposition to Him (37), and He will rule uninterrupted for ever without challenge (38).

Other Sons

However, to honour His Son, His Father is now bringing many sons to glory. They were all sharers in flesh and blood, and so Christ chose to take on their flesh and blood Himself (39). As a result they can now partake of His divine nature (40). This is possible because they have been rescued from the Devil's control by the victory of Christ at Calvary (41). They now belong to the Son, have become His companions, His 'fellows', His brethren. He is the firstborn among them, the greatest of them all (42). They can also become partakers of a heavenly calling, far beyond what they could aspire to naturally, to become those obedient people among whom God can live together now through the Holy Spirit. And for them, the Son now leads their praise to God in heaven itself (43).

What a privilege that we have been enabled to become companions of such a vastly superior Messiah-King-Priest. All glory goes to Him and to His God and Father!

References: (1) Phil.2:7 (2) Is.35:5-6 (3) Matt.11:2-10 (4) Rev.1:7 (5) Phil.2:10 (6) Phil.2:11 (7) Jn.1:41 (8) Matt.28:18 (9) 1 Cor.15:25 (10) Heb.3:5-6; 9:9 (11) Heb.4:8 (12) Heb.10:19,22 (13) Heb.7:11,19 (14) Heb.10:11-14 (15) Heb.12:22 (16) Is.6:1-2 (17) Matt.11:27 ESV (18) Heb.2:9 (19) 1 Pet.1:23-25 (20) Heb.1:8 (21) Ps.2:8; Heb.1:5 (22) Ps.97:7; Heb.1:6 (23) Rev.22:8-9 (24) 1 Tim.6:15 (25) Ps.93:2; Heb.1:8 (26) Ps.11:7; Heb.1:9 (27) Ps.45:4; Heb.1:8-9 (28) Jn.17:24 (29) Heb.1:5 ESV (30) Matt.3:17 (31) Matt.17:5 (32) Rom.1:4 (33) Heb.1:9 (34) Ps.102:25-27 (35) Heb.1:10-12

(36) Matt.28:18 (37) Ps.110:1; Heb.1:12 (38) Heb.1:8 (39) Heb.2:14 (40) 2 Pet.1:4 (41) Heb.2:14-15 (42) Rom.8:29; Heb.2:10-11 (43) Heb.2:10-13

Bible quotations from the NKJV, unless otherwise stated.

7

THE SERVING HIGH PRIEST (DAVID WEBSTER)

There are two priesthoods mentioned in the Old Testament of our Bibles. The first is that of Melchizedek who appears in Genesis 14. Abram had been forced into a war with four local kings who had taken his nephew Lot captive. We read:

"After Abram returned from defeating Kedorlaomer and the kings allied with him, the king of Sodom came out to meet him in the Valley of Shaveh (that is, the King's Valley). Then Melchizedek king of Salem brought out bread and wine. He was priest of God Most High, and he blessed Abram, saying, 'Blessed be Abram by God Most High, Creator of heaven and earth. And praise be to God Most High, who delivered your enemies into your hand.' Then Abram gave him a tenth of everything" (1).

Notice that there are no genealogical details to introduce us to Melchizedek - that's unusual. Also, he is both a king and a priest and he brought sustenance and blessing to Abram, known later as Abraham, one of the most important individuals in Bible history.

The second priesthood is the Levitical (or Aaronic) priesthood. This priesthood is exclusive to the tribe of Levi and from the family of Aaron. There was to be a perpetual priesthood by succession of the eldest son. We read in Exodus:

> *"Have Aaron ... brought to you from among the Israelites, along with his sons Nadab and Abihu, Eleazar and Ithamar, so they may serve me as priests. Make sacred garments for ... Aaron to give him dignity and honour ... Whenever Aaron enters the Holy Place, he will bear the names of the sons of Israel over his heart on the breastpiece of decision as a continuing memorial before the LORD ... The priesthood is theirs by a lasting ordinance"* (2).

Both of these priesthoods are important in understanding the role of the Lord Jesus as high priest. Melchizedek's role as priest is used to emphasise the permanent and eternal nature of the Lord Jesus as high priest whereas Aaron and his successors are often contrasted with the role of the Lord Jesus, while also providing us with a picture of what the Lord Jesus is doing for His people today.

It is Peter who tells us: *"you also, like living stones, are being built into a spiritual house to be a holy priesthood, offering spiritual sacrifices acceptable to God through Jesus Christ ... you are a chosen people, a royal priesthood, a holy nation"* (3). Just as God's Old Testament people were a kingdom of priests and a holy nation (4) so, in the present age, the spiritual house is to function as a priesthood. It is to the book of Hebrews that we look to find out all about that priesthood and the high priest who is serving in heaven for us.

Job Specification

The Bible teaches us: *"Every high priest is selected from among the people and is appointed to represent the people in matters related to God, to offer gifts and sacrifices for sins"* (5). It is important that the high priest came from the people he was to represent. Moses and Aaron were brothers, but lived in very different circumstances. Moses was brought up as the son of Pharaoh's daughter; in other words, he lived in luxury! Aaron remained with the people of Israel and was forced to work for the Egyptians. He had experienced the misery, affliction and suffering of those days of forced labour and cruel taskmasters! Moses, therefore, could never be appointed high priest.

Aaron, on the other hand, understood what the people went through and had suffered with them. Hebrews makes the point that we have one who has been tempted in every way, just as we are -yet he did not sin (6). Thus the Lord Jesus could personally relate to us in our struggles. It is also essential to this role that a high priest has something to offer (7). The offering of Himself and the acceptable sacrifice of Christ's blood makes it possible for us to serve the living God (8)! The Lord Jesus explained to a woman He met that God wants worshippers (9) - in Hebrews we are told how this comes to be, as we learn that we have confidence to enter the Most Holy Place by the blood of Jesus (10) and that we are encouraged to draw near to God with a sincere heart and with the full assurance that faith brings (11). Entering confidently into the presence of God, which was strictly forbidden under the Levitical system, is now a real possibility because of our High Priest.

Like Melchizedek

Firstly, the name Melchizedek means 'king of righteousness' and we are reminded that Melchizedek was king of Salem (12). Salem means peace. So righteousness and peace come together in this mysterious person, but, more significantly, in the Lord Jesus who has become for us wisdom from God— that is, our righteousness, holiness and redemption (13) and who is also our peace (14).

Secondly, in the written record, he is without father or mother, without genealogy, without beginning of days or end of life, resembling the Son of God, he remains a priest forever (15). Unlike the priests of Israel who grew old and died, this priest is permanent. We need not fear our Priest's deterioration or death! Thirdly, he was great! Abram was the great-grandfather of Levi and yet he gave a tithe to this great man and received a blessing from him. A great person is being blessed by a greater. Fourthly, he was both a priest and king. Psalm 110 is a prophecy about the Lord Jesus:

The LORD will extend your mighty sceptre from Zion, saying,
"Rule in the midst of your enemies!"
Your troops will be willing on your day of battle.
Arrayed in holy splendour, your young men will come to you like dew from
the morning's womb.
The LORD has sworn and will not change his mind:
"You are a priest forever, in the order of Melchizedek" (16).

Zechariah also wrote about a coming king-priest (17) a dual role only possible as a result of being designated a priest in the order of Melchizedek.

Like Aaron and His Successors

Hebrews tells us that the sanctuary that Moses constructed was only a copy of the true one in heaven (18). The work of the Levitical priests involved sacrifices and offerings made over and over again. In particular the high priest entered on the Day of Atonement, the tenth day of the seventh month of every year (19), into the Most Holy Place, a place otherwise forbidden, to offer sacrifices for himself and for the people. Only he was allowed to enter the Most Holy Place behind the curtain to stand before God. Having made a sacrifice for himself and for the people, he then brought the blood into the Most Holy place and sprinkled it on the atonement cover or mercy seat (20), where God lived in a special way. He did this to make atonement for himself and the people for all their sins committed during the year just ended. In the fulfilment of this, the Lord Jesus, as our High Priest, has entered heaven itself (21) once for all … by the sacrifice of himself (22) obtaining not just atonement for one year, but eternal redemption (23).

There was constant sin and that required constant sacrifice. There was deterioration and death and that required a new high priest every so often. By contrast, the Lord Jesus as high priest has entered once for all (not repeatedly) into heaven (24) (not an earthly copy of it), has sat down (25) (indicating a finished work), and is a forerunner (26) (indicating that we are to follow). There He intercedes for us: "Therefore he is able to save completely those who come to God through him" (27). In addition, because of the Lord Jesus' role as high priest we can approach God's throne of grace with confidence, so that we may receive mercy and find grace to help us in our time of need (28).

Just perfect!

Such a high priest truly meets our need - one who is holy, blameless, pure, set apart from sinners, exalted above the heavens (29). What more could we ask for?

References: (1) Gen.14:17-20 (2) Ex.28:1-2,29;29:9 (3) 1 Pet.2:5,9 (4) Ex.19:6 (5) Heb.5:1 (6) Heb.4:15 (7) Heb.8:3 (8) Heb.9:14 (9) John 4:23 (10) Heb. 10:19 (11) Heb.10:22 (12) Heb.7:2 (13) 1 Cor.1:30 (14) Eph.2:14 (15) Heb.7:3 (16) Ps.110:2-4 (17) Zech.6:12-13 (18) Heb.9:24 (19) Lev.23:26-27 (20) Lev.16:14-15 (21) Heb.9:24 (22) Heb.9:26 (23) Heb.9:12 (24) Heb.8:1; 9:24 (25) Heb.8:2; 10:12 (26) Heb.6:20 (27) Heb.7:25 (28) Heb.4:16 (29) Heb.7:26

Bible quotations from the NIV.

8

THE FAITHFUL SON OVER GOD'S HOUSE (STEPHEN MCCABE)

Hebrews 1 gloriously presents Jesus Christ as 'the Son' - the one through whom the Father has spoken definitively (1). The one who radiates the glory of God and is the exact expression of His nature (2). This is the One to whom God the Father has said: *"You are My Son, today I have begotten You"* (3) and again, *"I will be a Father to Him, and He shall be a Son to Me"* (4). A son speaks with all of the authority of his father and is the heir of all that belongs to him. The writer to the Hebrews is quoting words that God used long ago, and in a different way - an exploration of this will deepen our appreciation of what the Father has said to His unique Son.

The King as 'Son'

Psalm 2, quoted by the writer to the Hebrews, is the great coronation psalm of the king of Israel - that's how God's people would have understood it at the time. The psalmist depicts the nations raging around little Israel and saying that the Lord and His anointed have no authority over them (5). But God is in heaven, sovereign, and no matter what the nations are doing, God declares, *"I have installed my king upon Zion."* God

39

has placed the king of Israel in Jerusalem, His holy mountain. The king of Israel speaks in response: *"He [God] said to Me, 'You are my son, today I have become your father'"* (6). It is as if the great God of heaven is saying, "King of Israel, you speak with My authority to the earth. You are My son!" What a position the king of Israel was in!

It's exactly what God promised to David, concerning Solomon and those who followed after him: *"I will establish the throne of his kingdom forever. I will be a father to him and he will be a son to Me"* - God's great promise to the Davidic line in 2 Samuel 7:13-14. What a relationship between the king on the throne in Jerusalem and God! And so, it doesn't matter what the nations around about Israel are doing - God's chosen king sits in Jerusalem, invested with sonship, with the earth as his inheritance. Perhaps you can imagine the people cheering as the psalm is sung in a time of rejoicing at the coronation of the king!

The Holy Spirit has a fuller meaning for us to grasp in this coronation Psalm, because He takes it up and applies it to the Lord Jesus when the writer to the Hebrews repeatedly says that, although this was said in Psalm 2 to the king of Israel, God has said it again to His unique Son (7). Jesus is the King in God's kingdom, and the ultimate fulfilment of the father-son relationship seen depicted between God and the Davidic kings installed in Jerusalem. And as the King in God's kingdom today, the Son, He is the heir of all things, and He speaks with all of the authority of God the Father, in a way that those kings never could!

Greater Than David - Son and Lord

In Psalm 110, David states that, *"The LORD says to my Lord: 'Sit at My right hand, until I make Your enemies a footstool for Your feet'"* (8). Many centuries later, the Lord Jesus stumped the Pharisees, asking them, *"If*

David then calls Him 'Lord', how is He his son?" (9). How could David's descendent be greater than him? They couldn't answer Him that day. But the answer for us is found in Psalm 110 - *"Sit at My right hand ... Rule"* (10) - and Romans 1 – *"His Son, who was born a descendant of David according to the flesh, who was declared the Son of God with power by the resurrection from the dead"* (11).

Jesus was David's Son, a descendant of David, humanly speaking. But Paul says it was the resurrection from the dead that declared Him to be David's Lord - gloriously fulfilling the words of Psalm 110:1. The New Testament writers tell us on multiple occasions that these words of David are applied to the resurrection and ascension of the Lord Jesus Christ. So, for example, Peter says in Acts 2 that it wasn't David who ascended into heaven, but it was Jesus when the Father invited Him to "sit at My right hand" (12) This Davidic Son, then, is greater even than David - alive today and forever, and sitting at the right hand of the Majesty on high.

Greater Than Moses - Son Over God's House

Having expounded the uniqueness of Jesus as 'the Son', the writer to the Hebrews introduces us to a unique biblical phrase, declaring Jesus to be Son over His house (13) In doing this, the Lord Jesus is compared to, and shown to surpass by far, God's servant Moses (14). *"He is faithful in all My household; with him I speak mouth to mouth"* (15). At the time, God's house on earth was the Tabernacle - in what way was Moses faithful in relation to it? He was entrusted with God's design for His dwelling place - a design that, under the faithful supervision of Moses, was executed in every detail (16) leading to the awesome climactic statement that the glory of the LORD filled the tabernacle (17). It was the faithfulness of Moses in communicating God's design, and in following the procedures that God had outlined (for example, the commissioning of Aaron and his sons as priests (18) that allowed the functioning and service of God's dwelling-place in that day. What a privileged way for a mere man to demonstrate faithfulness!

But just as a builder is counted as having more honour than the house; just as the owner is greater than the servant, so the Lord Jesus surpasses Moses in our estimation - not simply servant, but faithful as Son (loaded with all our above considerations) over God's house today! Not the tabernacle of Moses' day, or even the subsequent temple in Jerusalem, but God's spiritual house (19). The work of the Lord Jesus, both in redemption at Calvary and today as our Great High Priest, has allowed the functioning and service of God's spiritual house in the here-and-now. Faithfully He serves in the holy place not made with hands (20), of which the holy place in the Tabernacle and Temple were mere copies (21), allowing the offering up of spiritual sacrifices acceptable to God through Him (22). Today we enjoy God's spiritual reality, with Jesus as Son over God's house - far surpassing the physical models of the Old Testament.

Royal Son and Priest Forever

The title of 'Son over God's house', therefore, uniquely refers to the Lord Jesus Christ, knitting together His kingship and His eternal priesthood as associated with the functioning and service of God's house (developed further in Hebrews 5:5-6). There again, alongside the Father's declaration. *"You are My Son,"* the writer returns to David's Messianic Psalm 110. The words are spoken to David's Son and Lord: *"The LORD has sworn and will not change His mind. 'You are a priest forever according to the order of Melchizedek'* (23).

This oath was made (to the one who was also declared to be *'My Son'*, installed in heavenly Zion when the Law was superseded following the death, resurrection and glorious ascension of the Lord Jesus (24), when God invited the Son to *"sit at My right hand."* King and Priest seen together in the Son over God's house, eternally - the one who has taken us from 'never' (25) to "forever' (26) in the service of God, having sat down at His right hand. An earlier chapter has already dealt with the figure of Melchizedek as foreshadowing these offices of the Lord Jesus Christ. It suffices here to say that it is evident in the very origins of His dealing with men and women in Scripture, that our God is committed to Calvary, as well as to the glories that follow; of the resurrection and ascension, and the offices bestowed on the Lord Jesus in bringing many to glory with the Son.

What Does It Mean for Me?

Today, our Lord Jesus Christ, Son over God's house, is in heavenly Zion - installed there as King, with all the authority of His Father, and appointed as glorious High Priest, to represent God's People in the things relating to God. That means that we should not be idle - we are under Him, conditionally, as the one over God's house (27) In seeking to serve faithfully in God's house today, we carry the message of the King to others (28) and also come through Him to offer spiritual sacrifices to God the Father, acceptable through our Great High Priest (29). He lives and serves faithfully today as Son over God's house so that we might be fully engaged in the service of God's house in a way that would be impossible without Him. Praise God!

References: (1) Heb.1:2 (2) Heb.1:3 (3) Heb.1:5 (4) Heb.1:5 (5) Ps.2:1-3 (6) Ps.2:6-7 NIV (7) Heb.1:5; 5:5; see also Acts 13:33 (8) Ps.110:1 (9) Matt.22:41-45 (10) Ps.110:1-2 (11) Rom.1:3-4 (12) Acts 2:32-35 (13) Heb.3:6 (14) Heb.3:3 (15) Num.12:7-8 (16) Ex.25-40 (17) Ex.40:34-35

(18) Ex.40:12-15 (19) 1 Pet.2:5 (20) Heb.8:1-2; 9:11 (21) Heb.9:24 (22) 1 Pet.2:5 (23) Ps.110:4 (24) Heb.7:28 (25) Heb.10:11 (26) Heb.10:12-14 (27) Heb.3:6 (28) 1 Pet.2:9-10 (29) 1 Pet.2:5; Heb.8:3

Bible quotations from the NASB, unless stated otherwise.

9

THE SUPERIOR MEDIATOR (DAVID VILES)

"Could Do Better ..."

Perhaps this phrase evokes uncomfortable memories from our school days, recalling room for improvement in matters sporting or academic. In the matter of divine covenants, however – the arrangements established by God to regulate His relationship with the human race – there could never be any need for improvement: *"his works are perfect, and all his ways are just"* (1). Nevertheless, we are assured more than once in the letter to the Hebrews that God – who Himself established the 'old' Covenant mediated by Moses with Israel – came to judge the law of that covenant to be very less than perfect, in fact weak and unprofitable (2).

The problem was not with God, whose foreknowledge envisioned the defects of the Old Covenant and provided for their rectification, but with the people of Israel and their failure to live up to their side of the arrangement, despite their initial enthusiasm – *"All that the LORD has said we will do"* (3). God could, and would, do better – through the New Covenant.

45

The Context

The question must therefore be asked, why did God take such infinite pains to uphold His Old Covenant with such a *"rebellious and stiff-necked people"* (4)? While we cannot presume to question the dictates of God's sovereign will, we are told that the Old Covenant was a temporary arrangement with a national focus. Its implications brought both glory and ultimate disaster (through disobedience) to the Israelite nation, but in God's ongoing purpose it was merely a stage – a *"tutor to bring us to Christ, that we might be justified by faith"* (5). In God's eternal plan, this narrow national focus was to be replaced with New Covenant blessings lavishly bestowed on all those (Jew and Gentile) so justified, under a covenant mediated by none other than Christ Himself.

Such an extension of God's purposes was challenging for Christians of Jewish descent, steeped in the nationalistic context of a glorious covenant which God declared nevertheless to be obsolete and ageing (6). The temptation, particularly under the prevailing persecution (7), to reintroduce a 'Jewish' gloss to their new lives in Christ, or even to revert to the security of Old Covenant practices, was strong and pervasive. It earned consistent opposition and a stinging rebuke from the Apostle Paul who had himself made the same spiritual journey to Christ – *"how is it that you are turning back to those weak and miserable principles ... to be enslaved by them all over again?"* (8).

By divine inspiration, the writer of the Hebrews epistle takes a less confrontational approach. We are privileged to be led by him into a presentation, in exalted and explicit detail, of the flawless facets of the New Covenant (9); like a precious jewel, he scrutinises it closely in comparison and contrast with the limitations of the Old. Glorious and exalted the Old Covenant undoubtedly was both in its inception and application, but, as Paul insisted, its glory is far eclipsed by that of the New Covenant because through it God did 'better' – the characteristic word of the Hebrews letter.

Better ... Best

In fact, we are confronted, not just with the comparative, but with the superlative. It is not only that the New Covenant is 'better' than the Old – it is 'perfect' (fulfilled, complete) because it is focused on a perfect High Priest, the Son of God (10). As he makes clear at the beginning of his argument, the writer has much to say about the priesthood of Christ (11). In a passage which must have left its original Jewish readers stunned by its Spirit-driven audacity, the writer emphasises that the claims of the Lord Jesus to high priestly status, so specially identified with, and reserved to, the descendants of Aaron in the Jewish mind, predated and surpassed the appointment even of Aaron himself (12).

The previous examined the superiority of the high priesthood of Christ in the royal order of Melchizedek. Suffice it to note here that Hebrews lays particular stress on the centrality of the divinely ordained priesthood to the nature of the covenant – *"when there is a change of the priesthood, there must also be a change of the law"* (13); the imperative is clear – a new priesthood means a new covenant. Centuries before, Korah and others had dared to aspire to the priesthood, rebelling against the authority of Moses and Aaron. Their punishment from God was as sudden as it was exemplary and it entered into the annals of Israel – *"that no outsider, who is not a descendent of Aaron, should come near to offer incense before the Lord"* (14). So there was neither a change in the priesthood nor (therefore) a change in the covenant at that time. The Hebrews epistle confirms that it is for no-one (not even the Son of God) to assume the position of priest for himself. God alone must ordain who is to be accorded this signal honour as He had done with Aaron and his sons (15), and God chose His Son to fulfil this New Covenant role – as a priest in the ancient Melchizedek order, not descended from mortal Aaron, but possessing indissoluble life (16).

Emphasising the importance of this change of priesthood and differentiating it sharply from what went before at Sinai, our writer is inspired to refer to two verses from the Psalms – short, but full of significance for the authority of our great High Priest. The first emphasises the Lord Jesus' fitness for this exalted office, as the eternally begotten Son of the Father (17). The second, repeated later in the epistle, stresses that His appointment was made on the basis of an irrevocable oath spoken by God Himself (18). It is most unusual for Scripture to refer to God in a way which links the finality and permanence attached (humanly speaking) to an oath (19) with the awesome nature of a divinely sworn statement, but such is the import of these verses. We are solemnised by what is being stated – God is binding Himself finally and permanently to the appointment of His Son as High Priest and, therefore, to the terms of the New Covenant of which He is the focus. As a result of this oath, His High Priest offers us 'gilt-edged collateral' – a full guarantee (surety) of the benefits of the New Covenant, because Christ is Himself that surety (20).

The Privileges of the New Covenant

With such a High Priest, such a Mediator, such a Surety, how can the New Covenant fail to be far 'better' for its beneficiaries than what went before? Human failure undermined the benefits of the Old, but the Lord Himself assures us that the New Covenant is founded upon His blood *"shed for many for the remission of sins"* (21). Nothing, not even human failure, can detract from the merits of that blood – it *"speaks for us before*

[God's] throne, proclaims redemption's work is done" (22). *"For this reason"* (23) – the authority of His own shed blood – Christ is the Mediator of the New Covenant.

This better sacrifice engenders *"better promises"* for the believer than were available under the Old Covenant. Hebrews redefines a striking prophecy of Jeremiah's – which will be applicable also to redeemed Israel in a future day – applying it to the foundational promises of the New Covenant: God's will inculcated in human hearts by the indwelling Spirit rather than imposed by external commandment, with the crowning assurance of God not only forgiving but forgetting our sins (24) and the guarantee (from the Mediator of the covenant Himself) of "the promised eternal inheritance" (25).

The intimacy with God implied by these better promises anticipates the most precious of the 'better things' identified in the epistle – "a better hope, through which we draw near to God" (26). Under the Old Covenant, that high privilege of access into God's most holy presence was available only once a year and only then through the representative high priest. In contrast, our hearts thrill to the divine invitation to draw near, with confidence, in worship – *"in full assurance of faith"* through the merits of that shed blood (27). Do we value this enormous opportunity as we should? To be welcomed into God's own sanctuary – a place of joy where we meet God and the Mediator Himself; the writer can only use terms which were precious to his hearers – Mount Zion, the heavenly Jerusalem (28) – to attempt to describe this place, the glory of which transcends our understanding.

In telling contrast is the fearful and terrible meeting place of Sinai, where a holy God initiated the Old Covenant relationship, glorious as it was (29)! Through the Mediator of the New Covenant, our access is very far 'better' – in fact, 'perfect.'

References: (1) Deut.32:4 NIV (2) Heb.7:18 (3) Ex.24:7 (4) Deut.31:27 NIV (5) Gal.3:24 (6) Heb.8:13 (7) Heb.12:3–7 (8) Gal.4:9 NIV (9) 2 Cor.3:7–11 (10) Heb.7:11 (11) Heb.5:11 (12) Heb.7:1–16 (13) Heb.7:12 NIV (14) Num.16:40 (15) Ex.28:1; Heb.5:4–5 (16) Heb.7:16 (17) Ps.2:7; Heb.5:5 (18) Ps.110:4; Heb.5:6; 7:20–21,28 (19) Cf. Heb.6:16–17 (20) Heb.7:22 (21) Matt.26:28 (22) J.B. Belton – O Lord Thy Courts We Humbly Tread, PHSS 99 (23) Heb.9:15 (24) Heb.8:8–12 (25) Heb.9:15 NIV (26) Heb.7:19 (27) Heb.10:19–23 (28) Heb.12:22–24 (29) Heb.12:18–21

All Bible references from the NKJV, unless stated otherwise.

10

THE FORERUNNER (BRIAN FULLARTON)

"... behind the veil, where the forerunner has entered for us, even Jesus, having become High Priest forever ..." (Heb.6:19–20).

To understand the meaning of the word 'forerunner' in Hebrews 6:20, we have to bear in mind that the Lord Jesus always in His earthly life had the thought of a future day before Him, following His perfect sacrifice and preparation for His unique high priestly activity, when an expectant and eager people (the 'us' of verse 20) would be in readiness to do service to God in spiritual worship, having firmly laid hold of 'the hope' set before them (v.18). This surely has to do with the collective approach of a people to God in His sanctuary, dependent, as was Israel in the past, on the pre-entrance of their high priest into the most holy place (also called 'the Holiest of All'(1)) in the earthly sanctuary, but with two major differences:

(a) Israel's priestly representative alone made his way into the most holy part of the tabernacle without any later accompaniment by the people on whose behalf he was acting; (2) moreover, he was only there for a very limited time.

(b) The purpose of Aaron's entrance and service, as high priest, on one specific day of the year in Israel's calendar, was to make atonement with the blood of the sin offering, first for himself and then for God's people, whom he was representing.

In the case of the Lord Jesus, His entry fully opened the way for His people to follow directly into the very presence of God – the Majesty in the heavens – where He is seated at His Father's right hand (3). He is there constantly in His Father's presence. When we come in worship, that's where we are; exactly where He is (4).

Then again, He is not in the true tabernacle above to make atonement for our sins; He did that gloriously on the basis of His sacrifice at Calvary. His service is important in leading His people in praise and worship, at which time in that heavenly place He still speaks worthily of the Father to our hearts as we are engaged in meditation and adoration, and joyfully proclaims His Father's glories and attributes in song with perfect pitch and tone (5).

The Tabernacle: The Way of Approach to God

When we consider the layout of the Mosaic tabernacle, that magnificent structure of the dwelling place of Almighty God on earth, and in particular the location within it where He would directly communicate with His servant Moses, we can understand the long period of time Moses willingly spent in the mountain in Sinai. He was 'with God' forty days and nights, learning everything that had to be learned – "According to all that I show you ..." (6).

It is unsurprising that such detail is so minutely recorded, for there are so many lessons to be taught from the significance of every item of furniture mentioned. Their existence, focus and purpose is to give us a fuller and greater understanding of the excellencies of the Son of God. Above all, the inner chamber of God's holy presence was to be the place of the highest privilege and fellowship that could be experienced by an earthly mortal (7). However, skilfully woven and brilliantly coloured curtains, standing wooden boards with horizontally fixed bars, in addition to the dividing veil between the holy place and the most holy place (8), ensured that the way of approach was no mere ramble. Each step of the journey in coming to God had to be carefully considered; after all, this was the Lord's own master-plan.

The ritual necessary in coming before God is emphasised in the preparation of the holy garments that had to be worn by the high priest. These garments reflected God's glory and the beautiful service which His chosen representative could undertake (9). Elaborate touches of jewellery adorned the head and body of the high priest in his daily priestly ministry to God for His nation (10). Close attention had to be paid to the demanding minutiae of the sacrificial system, all of which pointed forward to that one supreme self-sacrifice of the Son (11). We can readily imagine on that great Day of Atonement, 'Yom Kippur' (12), the whole camp of Israel would be at a standstill. No person was allowed to go near the tent of meeting. They couldn't see where exactly Aaron was, never mind what he was doing, after he made his way into the first compartment, the Holy Place. Then, after changing into his simple linen garments, he went on through the intervening veil into the holiest of all, all the while serving in silence. No such repetitions are needed today in this age of divine grace.

The All-important Passage of Hebrews 10:19-23

Many Christians today are missing out on the great truth unfolded in the narrative above. The setting for this climax of earthly, but sanctified human activity in divine/ heavenly service has to do with the responsibility of brothers and sisters (13) in the house of God, in and over which the Lord Jesus is a great priest (14). Corporate divine service assumes our coming and being together in churches of God (15), carrying out the word and will of God, all part of what is described as "the confession of our hope" (16); that is our assurance and conviction that we are where God wants us to be in testimony for Him, and defending and propagating what He has revealed to us concerning the faith (17). Unlike the nation of Israel, we ourselves fully enter in to the presence of God in worship, through the veil, that is spoken of as the blood-stained offering of Jesus' body – His flesh – in sacrificial death for us (18). It is all there for us to grasp and enjoy such a wonderful blood-bought privilege, week by week, for the rest of our earthly lives.

What now?

How sad it would be, if He is there in God's presence – as He most certainly is – waiting for us to come to worship on the first day of the week (19), and we are not there because of our possible deliberate physical absence. The voice of the worshipper rings out clearly and appealingly: Praise is awaiting You, O God, in Zion … (20). Oh come let us sing to the Lord! Let us shout joyfully to the Rock of our salvation. Let us come before His presence with thanksgiving; Let us shout joyfully to Him with psalms … Oh come, let us worship and bow down: Let us kneel before the Lord our Maker. For He is our God, and we are the people of His pasture, and the sheep of His hand (21). We come to the Remembrance to celebrate the Lord's death, eat the Lord's supper, and be at the Lord's table (22) – what a wonderful opportunity is ours!

References: (1) Heb.9:3 (2) Ex.30:10; Heb.9:7 (3) Heb.8:1;9:24 (4) Heb.10:19–22 (5) Heb.2:12 (6) Ex.25:9 (7) Ex.25:22 (8) Ex.26:1,15,26,33 (9) Ex.28:2 (10) Ex.28:6–43 (11) Ex.29 (12) Lev.16 (13) Heb.10:19 - although the masculine adelphos is used the word also has a wider meaning of those who share in a common heritage or origin (14) Heb.10:21 RV (15) Heb.10:25; 1 Cor.11:16–18,20,22; 14:23 (16) Heb.10:23 (17) Jude 3; 1 Tim.1:19b; 3:9; 2 Tim.3:8; 4:7 (18) Heb.10:20 (19) Acts 20:7 (20) Ps.65:1a (21) Ps.95:1–2,6–7 (22) 1 Cor.11:20,26; 10:21

Bible quotations from the NKJV, unless otherwise stated.

11

THE SEATED PURIFIER OF SINS (DON WILLIAMSON)

The writers in this book have been presenting the wonders of our exalted Christ. He is the eternal Son of God, the one appointed heir of all things, the one through whom the worlds are made! Hebrews 1:3 reveals: *"He is the radiance of God's glory, and the exact representation of God's nature."* Can we ever understand or truly appreciate the scriptural statement that says, 'He upholds all things by the word of His power'? Our Saviour is the exalted one; none can compare with Him, and it is in this context that we are to consider the fact that He is the purifier of sins.

Purification of the Flesh

In order to appreciate what our Lord Jesus has done for us it might be good to see what was required by God in Old Testament times for dealing with this issue of sin. We actually find one of the best explanations in the New Testament, in the book of Hebrews: *"For if the blood of goats and bulls, and the sprinkling of defiled persons with the ashes of a heifer, sanctify for the purification of the flesh, how much more will the blood of Christ, who through the eternal Spirit offered himself without blemish to God, purify our*

56

conscience from dead works to serve the living God" (1). Sin has been the separator from the beginning of time. God's provision for dealing with it in order for man to continue to have a relationship with Him was the offering of sacrifices (from a pure heart), resulting in "the purification of the flesh." This was to be at a cost to the one who had sinned and of course, it was the ultimate cost to the sacrifice that was offered in place of the sinner.

The power in the verse of Hebrews that we read is seen in the contrast of the sacrifices of the past to the one who is our once-for-all sacrifice. We get to consider the words, 'how much more'. There is no comparison between the one who is the purifier of sins and the possibly millions of animal sacrifices offered in the past. As I have already stated, there is none to compare with Him! This is what brings us to the point of wonder, that one of such exalted place should lower Himself to face the judgment and punishment due to us, so that we can serve God as those who have been cleansed.

Refined by Fire

I'm sure we can all understand the fact that some things are refined or purified by fire. While water is the usual symbol of cleansing, fire can be too; John's comments about the Lord baptizing in fire may illustrate this (2); and there is also the passage that commanded the Israelites to: "purify yourselves and your captives ..." and all articles "... everything that can stand the fire, you shall pass through the fire ... And whatever cannot stand the fire, you shall pass through the water" (3).

Although there are many metals that go through this process to reach their highest quality of purification, the best example might be gold. In order to secure the quality and high price of gold all foreign particles must be removed, and it is the application of fire that separates the pure gold from all the rest. Perhaps Peter had this cleansing in mind, when commenting on the practical outworking of the purification the Lord accomplishes (4). The Lord acknowledges this process in an illustrative point to the Church in Laodicea. "You say, I am rich, I have prospered, and I need nothing, not realizing that you are wretched, pitiable, poor, blind, and naked. I counsel you to buy from me gold refined by fire, so that you may be rich, and white garments so that you may clothe yourself ..." (5).

The saints in Laodicea had missed the mark, as they were neither hot nor cold toward God, but rather they were lukewarm. In fact, they were content to say that they were rich in this world's goods and therefore needed nothing. Yet the reality was they were spiritually poor and if they were to become truly rich they were to buy from Him spiritual riches refined by fire and white righteous garments of spiritual living. The riches of a man are what he is and does rather than what he has. The Lord knew all about the cost of the refining process and still He was willing to go through the pain and suffering of Calvary knowing that He would face the fierce judgment from a holy God and shed His blood so that you and I might have the purification of our sins.

Some of you may have heard of the forest fires in Colorado during a recent summer. We have had fires every year so in some ways it was not new, but this time the winds pushed the fire into a large city and the result was 365 homes being burnt to the ground. As I drove past the city that night on my way back to Littleton from Trinidad, I was awestruck with the sight of the fires on the side of the hills and on the edge of the city as house after house exploded in flame. A few days later, with the fires out, photos showed the total devastation and destruction that was left behind. Empty driveways and concrete foundations were all that were remaining in an entire neighbourhood. It is a reminder of the purging power of fire. This book aims to bring into our consciousness a fresh appreciation of Christ as the preeminent one without peer (6) and, at the same time, rejoicing that we have a relationship with Him by grace.

Who Has Sat Down on High

The statement in Hebrews takes us from Christ being the purifier of sins to being the one who has *"sat down ... on high."* When we are contemplating the person and work of the Lord Jesus, we should always remember that our Saviour is the ultimate victor! Think for a moment about the other religions of this world. Mohammad was a prophet, but he is dead and buried; Buddhism encompasses a variety of traditions, beliefs and practices largely based on teachings attributed to Siddhartha Gautama, who is commonly known as the Buddha, a man who has also died. And many of the cults like Mormonism and Jehovah's Witnesses all follow men who have died. You and I serve a living Saviour, one who has conquered sin, death and Satan's power and is now at the right hand of the throne of the Majesty in heaven (7)!

The description we are considering is one of position and authority, and from the view of a completed work. This should thrill our hearts as we realise the place the Lord occupies in the heavens for us, knowing that He is there as our High Priest, a minister in the holy places on our behalf. What a transformational change from sacrifice to High Priest!

As we think in awe of our Lord and Saviour, it would be good to go back and focus for a moment on the saints in Laodicea. The Lord said He would 'spit them out of His mouth' for being lukewarm (8). It must have grieved the Lord's heart, knowing the place He had left to come for men, the place He took on our behalf and the place of His ascended power. But He says to them, "Those whom I love, I reprove and discipline, so be zealous and repent … The one who conquers, I will grant him to sit with Me on My throne, as I also conquered and sat down with My Father on His throne" (9).

Wow! What a Saviour we have, one who by His grace has saved us from the eternal fire of judgement, purifies us for service before God, and seeks to share with us His glorious throne! Can we compare the riches of this world with Him? May we all seek to buy (for it will cost us time and convenience) of His gold, and to put on the garments of His holiness, for we are to be holy as He is holy (10). "He who has an ear, let him hear what the Spirit says to the churches" (11).

References: (1) Heb.9:13-14 (2) Lk.3:16; cf. Mk.10:38-39 (3) Num.31:19-23 (4) 1 Pet.1:3-9 (5) Rev.3:17-18 (6) Col.3:15-20 (7) Heb.8:1 (8) Rev.3:16 (9) Rev.3:19-21 (10) 1 Pet.1:16 (11) Rev.3:22

Bible quotations from the ESV.

12

THE PLEADING ADVOCATE (STEPHEN MCCABE)

"We have an advocate with the Father, Jesus Christ the righteous" (1 Jn.2:1).

An advocate speaks on behalf of, or represents, another. Paul's letter to Philemon is such a beautiful picture of advocacy. Paul's pleading there is on behalf of the servant, Onesimus, to Philemon, his master. It is surely like our Lord and Master who pleads for us, His servants, when we, in our own strength, fall so easily into sin.

'... my child ...' (1)

Paul refers to Onesimus as his child. You may remember how Joseph brought Ephraim and Manasseh before Jacob (2). It's a faint echo of the Lord bringing the fruit of His work before His Father. Jacob says, "I never expected to see your face; and behold, God has let me see your offspring also" (3). Jesus, as advocate, presents us to His Father, the triumph of Calvary won, the horror of Calvary behind Him. Not only has the Father seen the face of the Son again, but He has seen those He has brought with Him – His offspring. When He speaks to the Father on our behalf, it is in the context of our being intimately associated with Him because we are His.

'... my very heart ...' (4)

Paul says that he is sending Onesimus, his very heart. The advocacy of Paul here, and more importantly, the advocacy of the Lord Jesus, is not a cold, detached thing. The word 'advocate' easily brings an image of courtroom drama to our minds with its legal association in our language. It is easy to picture a lawyer representing a client, where the lawyer leaves work to go home and leaves the case and its concerns in the office, forgets the client until he returns. But when the Lord Jesus speaks for us before the Father, remember that we are His very heart.

'... was useless, but now useful ...' (5)

Onesimus means 'useful', so Paul is starting his appeal to Philemon with a bit of a pun. But the point is serious – Onesimus could be useful to Philemon! Isn't it wonderful to think that we can be useful to the Father? Once we were useless, but now the Lord Jesus as advocate can recommend us before the Father. How useful are we actually being? It's very easy, as part of a church, to just drift along under the radar. If too many people in an assembly start doing that then the church loses direction. It would be awful to contemplate a church of God – a group of people called together to serve God in His house – becoming unprofitable to God. Let's not allow that to happen in our churches! We were once useless to God, but now we can be useful to Him through what Jesus has done – let's make sure we are.

'... receive him as you would receive me ...' (6)

What a beautiful thing for Paul to say. And he is asking a lot! Philemon knew Paul. He respected and loved him. Paul says, "For my sake, do the exact same for Onesimus." The Father loves the Son more completely than we can presently understand. The Lord Jesus speaks on our behalf to the Father – "Receive him, receive her, as you would receive me." Elsewhere Paul says that we are "accepted in the Beloved" (7). There is no more wonderful position to be in than that.

'... whatever he owes, put that on my account – I will repay ...' (8)

Onesimus is very likely to have stolen from Philemon, but Paul says that he will 'foot the bill'. The big difference in what the Lord Jesus does for us is that He has already paid. The old account was settled long ago. So whenever the accuser, Satan, stands before God to point the finger (9), there is one who speaks on my behalf – "That has been paid for, paid for by My own blood, My own life." Our advocate says, "Whatever he or she owes, that was put on My account. And it has been settled." The great comfort of 1 John 2:1 is that if and when we do sin, and our potentially useful service for our Master is put at risk, we have one who speaks for us before God, so we have nothing to fear.

References: (1) Phm.1:10 (2) Gen.48:1,9 (3) Gen.48:11 (4) Phm.1:12 (5) Phm.1:11 (6) Phm.1:17 (7) Eph.1:6 NKJV (8) Phm.1:18-19 (9) Zech.3:1; Rev.12:10

Bible quotations from the ESV, unless otherwise stated.

13

THE ETERNAL SON OF GOD (GEORGE PRASHER)

God's nature and being are beyond our full understanding, but like David we can say: *"Lord, my heart is not haughty, nor mine eyes lofty; neither do I exercise myself in great matters, nor in things too wonderful for me"* (Ps.131:1). Learning to accept all that God has revealed in Scripture, we take on trust those aspects of truth which are beyond human comprehension. This attitude helps us when we consider the excellency of the Lord Jesus Christ as the eternal Son of God. For He did not become the Son of God when He was born of Mary in Bethlehem. He had been the Son of the Father from everlasting: this was an eternal relationship within the Godhead.

Let me remind you of two verses in John's first epistle: *"... we have seen, and bear witness, and declare unto you the life, the Eternal, which was with the Father and hath been manifested unto us; that which we have seen and heard declare we unto you also, that ye also may have fellowship with us: yea and our fellowship is with the Father, and with His Son"* (1:3). Now the One who is here described as the Eternal, which was with the Father, and was manifested unto us, could only be the Son. Therefore the relationship of

Father and Son was eternal. There was no time in eternity past when He became the Son of God. He had always been the Son of the Father. This of course shows the unique nature of the relationship, but does not imply that the Father existed before the Son. It is not used in the same sense as when we speak of a human father and son. Colossians 2:9 tells us that in Christ dwells all the fulness of the Godhead bodily - He therefore shares with the Father all that belongs to Deity, including the fact that God is from everlasting to everlasting.

Isaiah foretold that the virgin would conceive and bear a son whose name would be Immanuel, which means, God is with us (Isaiah 7:14). Of this wondrous Person the prophet Micah also wrote, informing us that He would be born in Bethlehem, and that His goings forth were, *"from of old, from everlasting"* (Mic.5:2). There is a most interesting reference to Christ as Son in the second Psalm in which David was moved by the Holy Spirit to write: *"Serve the Lord with fear, and rejoice with trembling. Kiss the Son, lest He be angry, and ye perish in the way ... Blessed are all they who put their trust in Him"* (vv.11,12).

The Son is so great that all are urged to make their peace with Him: and all are blessed who have put their trust in Him. Of whom could such things be said, but of One who is divine? That this is indeed a reference to the Lord Jesus as the eternal Son of God is confirmed by the earlier statement made in the Psalm: *"I will tell of the decree: The Lord said unto Me, Thou art My Son; this day have I begotten Thee. Ask of Me, and I will give Thee the nations for Thine inheritance, and the uttermost parts of the earth for Thy possession"* (v.7).

Three times in the New Testament, this decree is quoted as referring to the Lord Jesus (Heb.1:5; 5:5; Acts 13:33). We should clearly understand, of course, that the statement "this day have I begotten Thee" does not mean a particular point in time, but expresses a relationship between God the Father and God the Son which is altogether unique. It was the Lord Himself who spoke in John 10:36 of the Father sanctifying Him and sending Him into the world: "If He called them gods unto whom the word of God came (and the Scripture cannot be broken), say ye of Him whom the Father sanctified and sent into the world, Thou blasphemest; because I said, I am the Son of God?"

Before His birth in Bethlehem, the Father sanctified or consecrated the Son for His great mission of redemption. The Father sent the Son to be the Saviour of the world. So that when His birth was announced to Mary, Gabriel said to her: "that which is to be born shall be called holy, the Son of God" (Lk.1:35). Only as we appreciate something of this wonderful, eternal relationship between God the Father and God the Son can we really enter into the excellency of our Saviour as the Son of God. The apostle John made this point when he wrote: "The Word became flesh, and dwelt among us (and we beheld His glory, glory as of the only begotten from the Father), full of grace and truth" (Jn.1:14).

Those to whom Christ was so revealed in the days of His flesh were privileged to see in Him an exact representation of the character of the Father. All that the Father was, He was. As He said to Philip on one occasion, "he that hath seen Me hath seen the Father" (John 14:9). And in a similar sense He is described in Colossians 1:15 as "the image of the invisible God." How altogether wonderful it is that this glorious Person should be my Saviour! "The Son of God, who loved me, and gave Himself up for me."

14

THE DIVINE CREATOR (GEORGE PRASHER)

The first sentence of our Bible tells us: *"In the beginning God created the heaven and the earth."* Answering to this, we read in the first verses of John's gospel: *"In the beginning was the Word, and the Word was with God, and the Word was God ... All things were made by Him; and without Him was not anything made that hath been made"* (vv.1,3). It is clear that the One spoken of as the Word is the Lord Jesus for in verse 14 we are told that *"the Word became flesh and dwelt among us."* What then do we learn from the fact that all things were made by Him, when we know from the verse in Genesis that God created the heaven and the earth? The word for God in Genesis 1:1 is Elohim, a plural Hebrew word form meaning more than two. Showing that, as later revealed in Scripture, God the Father, God the Son and God the Holy Spirit were all involved in the planning and process of creation.

The prominent part played by the Lord Jesus is made clear in Paul's letter to the Colossians. Speaking of Christ as the Son of God's love, Paul wrote: *"For in Him were all things created, in the heavens and upon the earth, things visible and things invisible, all things have been created through Him and unto Him; and He is before all things and in Him all things consist"* (Col.1:16).

67

These words impress upon us the vast range of Christ's creative works. They were created in Him, for He was the Centre of divine counsels before creation, the Architect and Mathematician of the universe. *"Through Him"* marks out our Lord as Himself the One who brought creation into existence. He was the "Master Workman" as we are told in Proverbs chapter 8. *"Unto Him"* reminds us that it was for His glory that the universe was brought into being.

Then follows the wonderful statement that in Him *"all things consist,"* or *"hold together"* (RV margin) – He is the source of dynamic power by which matter coheres and the universe is regulated and controlled. We do well to think often about our Saviour as Creator. For by this we can better measure His greatness, wisdom, power and love. The immensity of the universe and its clockwork precision tell of His infinite power and wisdom. The loveliness of sunset, countryside and sea coast express His glory, the beauty of His mind. Each tiny insect or flower is exquisite in design. As the Psalmist said: "O LORD, how manifold are Thy works! In wisdom Thou hast made them all: the earth is full of Thy riches" (Ps.104:24).

The greatness and condescension of the Lord Jesus are beautifully expressed by the hymn writer:

> "In His own hands He holds the seas.
> He guides the tide, controls the breeze;
> The frost, the snow, the ice, the cold,
> Are all by His great power controlled;
> And yet an infant Babe He lay,
> In Bethlehem's manger on that day."
> (C.M. Luxmoore 1858–1922)

Yes, He was in the world, and the world was made by Him. To outward appearance He was an ordinary Man, eating and drinking, living in lowly circumstances among others - among those who were His creatures. But though found in fashion as a Man in this world He was declared to be the Son of God with power (Rom.1:4). He changed water into wine; restored sightless eyes; raised the dead; fed 5000 from two small fish and five barley loaves, and calmed the raging sea with a word.

> "Whether the wrath of the storm tossed sea,
> Or demons, or men, or whatever it be,
> No waters can swallow the ship where lies
> The Master of the ocean, and earth, and skies:
> They all shall sweetly obey My will, Peace, be still!"
> (Mary Ann Baker 1831-1921)

We find it hard to grasp how the Creator could become Man and dwell in this world. But God's word clearly reveals this to have been so, and as we accept it by faith the Holy Spirit helps us to treasure in our hearts the wonder of such grace and love. And how amazing that One so great should humble Himself even unto death, yes, the death of the cross!

> "Well might the sun in darkness hide.
> And shut its glories in,
> When the incarnate Maker died
> For man, His creature's sin."
> (Isaac Watts 1674-1748)

It was by this means, however, that He gloriously made possible a new creation. The old order had been spoiled by human sin and it is on the ground of the great Creator's sacrifice at Calvary that we who believe in Him are new creatures in Christ Jesus. *"For we are His workmanship, created in Christ Jesus for good works"* (Eph.2:10).

Nor is this all. We who believe are but the first fruits of a new creation. Divine purpose is moving forward to the great goal of a new heaven and a new earth. *"And He that sitteth on the throne said, behold I make all things new"* (Rev.21:5). About this Peter wrote: *"But according to His promise, we look for new heavens and a new earth, wherein dwelleth righteousness. Wherefore, beloved, seeing that ye look for these things, give diligence that ye may be found in peace, without spot and blameless in His sight"* (2 Pet.3:13,14).

15

THE ANOINTED AND RETURNING KING
(GEORGE PRASHER)

It's remarkable that a king should be born in a stable and cradled in a manger. Such a birthplace would have seemed to be too poor for any king. But the Lord Jesus was not only the King of the Jews and their rightful Messiah. He was also the King of the Ages, the eternal King of kings and Lord of lords.

> "He held the highest place above.
> Adored by all the sons of flame,
> But such His self-denying love,
> He laid aside His crown and came
> To seek the lost,
> And at the cost
> Of heavenly rank and earthly fame,
> He sought me. Blessed be His Name!"
> (E.A. Tydeman 1842-1914)

Looking at the infant King in Bethlehem's manger we remember the matchless grace of our Lord Jesus Christ. *"Though He was rich, for our* sakes He became poor, that we through His poverty might become rich" (2 Cor.8:9). The prophet Zechariah had written: "Rejoice greatly, O daughter of Zion, shout, O daughter of Jerusalem: behold thy King cometh unto thee: He is just and having salvation; lowly, and riding upon an ass, even upon a colt the foal of an ass" (Zech.9:9). These words were fulfilled when Jesus borrowed the colt of an ass on which to ride into Jerusalem just shortly before He died. All Jerusalem was stirred as the multitudes acclaimed Him. "Hosanna to the Son of David", they cried, "Blessed is He that cometh in the Name of the Lord; hosanna in the highest" (Matt.21:9).

The eternal King was riding on a lowly beast into Jerusalem, the city of the great King. Among the outstanding beauties of Christ's character were His meekness and His lowliness of heart, and to you and me as His disciples come His words: "Take My yoke upon you, and learn of Me; for I am meek and lowly in heart: and ye shall find rest unto your souls" (Matt.11:29). As witnesses in the world today, we are called upon to serve Him in this spirit. To us there will be given rest of soul in His service, and to others there will be given an impression of the lowly Christ which will commend our Saviour to them.

Israel's spiritual leaders should have recognized their King from what the prophets had written concerning Him, but they were blind through unbelief. So they urged the Roman Governor, Pontius Pilate to crucify the Lord of glory. Pilate was perplexed. He knew that Jesus had done nothing worthy of death. Yet for fear of his political future he was afraid to risk offending the Jewish leaders. He tried in various ways to release Jesus. Hoping to stir pity in the hearts of the accusers he took Jesus and scourged Him - a fearful ordeal for Christ, fulfilling the prophetic word which said: "I gave My back to the smiters, and My cheeks to them that plucked off the hair: I hid not My face from shame and spitting" (Is.50:6).

"The soldiers plaited a crown of thorns, and put it on His head, and arrayed Him in a purple garment; and they came unto Him, and said, Hail, King of the Jews! and they struck Him with their hands" (Jn.19:2,3). Then He was brought out before the Jews, to whom Pilate said, *"Behold, I bring Him out to you, that ye may know that I find no crime in Him"*; *"Behold your King!"* (Jn.19:4,14). *"Away with Him, away with Him, crucify Him,"* they cried. *"Shall I crucify your King?"* asked Pilate. The chief priests answered, "We have no king but Caesar." Then Pilate delivered Jesus unto them to be crucified, and Jesus went out bearing the cross for Himself, out to Golgotha, the place of the skull, and there they crucified Him. Over His head was written His accusation: "Jesus of Nazareth the King of the Jews." Shall we in thought sit and watch Him there for a few moments? Shall we try again to measure the love of our Saviour? Though infinite in power, He remained bound to the cross - bound in love for you and me!

> "And when He hung upon the tree,
> They wrote this Name above Him:
> That all might see the reason we
> For evermore must love Him."
> (George W. Bethune 1805–1862)

"Wherefore also God highly exalted Him, and gave unto Him the Name which is above every name: that in the name of Jesus every knee should bow" (Phil.2:9,10). As believers our faith rests on this assurance from God's word. God's great decree, however, stands firm, awaiting fulfilment despite all appearances to the contrary: *"Yet I have set My King upon My holy hill of Zion"* (Ps.2:6). God will give Him the nations for His inheritance and the uttermost parts of the earth for His possession, as the psalmist tells us. Among so much sadness, oppression and misrule in today's world, we may sometimes feel like another psalmist who cried, *"O LORD, how long?"*

To the natural mind it seems strange that God should so long permit the mismanagement of this world to continue under the control of failing men. But a thousand years in God's sight *"are but as yesterday when it is past, and as a watch in the night"* (Ps.90:4). The return to this world of His appointed king is certain, and we believe that more than ever before the signs of the times point towards the approach of this great crisis. As believers in Christ we await His return to the air to take from the world His Church. Beyond that wonderful event lies the time of the end – the most fearful epoch in all human history: a reign of terror by the Antichrist which will be brought to an end by the direct intervention of Christ Himself. This intervention is dramatically described in the book of Revelation:

> *"And I saw the heaven opened: and behold a white horse and He that sat thereon, called Faithful and True ... and the armies which are in heaven followed Him on white horses... And out of His mouth proceedeth a sharp sword, that with it He should smite the nations: and He shall rule them with a rod of iron ... and on His garment and on His thigh a name written, King of kings, and Lord of lords"* (Rev.19:11-16).

For a thousand years the Lord Jesus will reign in this world, as Revelation chapter 20 confirms. It will be the earth's Jubilee! Oppression will be vanquished, all warfare will be suppressed, all economic problems will be solved. In Psalm 72 we are given a remarkable impression of that coming golden age: *"In His days shall the righteous flourish; and abundance of peace, till the moon be no more ... all kings shall bow down before Him; all nations shall serve Him ... there shall be abundance of corn in the earth ... men shall be blessed in Him; all nations shall call Him blessed ... Blessed be the LORD the God of Israel ... and blessed be His glorious Name for ever; and let the whole earth be filled with His glory"* (vv.7,11,16,17-19).

Let us lay well to heart the Bible's unmistakeable message – mere human effort, however skilled or well intended, will never solve the world's problems. God's answer to the world's deep dilemma is Jesus Christ, His anointed King. Hasten the day when, as Isaiah tells us, our eyes *"shall see the King in His beauty"*!

16

THE APOSTLE OF OUR CONFESSION (BRIAN JOHNSTON)

The exhortation to consider Jesus as the Apostle was originally given to Jewish Christians who were in spiritual danger. They needed to be warned not to drift, fall or be carried away. What was the problem? They were leaning back toward the Law, and, in the process, their hearts were becoming hardened. In warning, the writer recalls to them the provocation Israel caused God by its hardening of heart on account of the lack of water at Rephidim (Ex.17:1). In that regard we read specifically of the temptation (Heb.3:8). Israel put God to the test by asking in particular: *"Is the LORD among us, or not?"* Instead of trusting God for help in adverse circumstances, they demanded a miracle to reveal His Presence.

Both in the letter to the Hebrews (3:7) and in Psalm 95 (verse 7) which was being cited, we find the expression *"His voice."* The Old Testament is referring to Jehovah's voice; while in Hebrews it is in the context of God speaking in His Son. How unmistakably the Spirit of God underlines for us the fact that Jehovah the Lord of the Old Testament is Jesus the Apostle and Messiah of the New Testament, the One through whom God has spoken to us, and whom these Jews were to consider.

The word "consider" as found in the RV carries the force of "to consider attentively" or, as the NIV renders it, "to fix your thoughts on." This again brings us to the danger these people were in. They had been allowing their attention to wander, so that their gaze was slowly turning back to the Law. To deliver themselves they must set their minds on Jesus, firstly as the Apostle. The term "apostle" conveys the idea of sending someone off on a commission to do something, having furnished him with credentials. In the Greek version of the Old Testament, the verb from the same word is used of God sending Moses. In this letter the writer, by the Spirit, compares the two apostles of the eras of the Law and Grace.

Viewed as the Apostle, Jesus is the One who came out from the Presence of God in order to bring God's Word to us. Previously, the prophets had brought God's Word to His people, but in the first chapter of Hebrews we are caused to consider Jesus the Apostle as the heir of all things, as the Creator of the worlds, as the brightness of eternal glory, as the expression of the divine essence, as the sustainer of the universe, and as the sacrifice that purges (a people) from sin. In these ways, the superiority of Jesus as the Apostle is set before us. We contrast, in passing, the fading, reflected glory that radiated from the face of Moses the apostle of the Law, as compared with the unfading, inherent, surpassing glory possessed by our Apostle.

God has spoken to us. The eternal Son, from Godhead's fullest glory, was the One whom the Father sanctified and sent into the world to bring us His Word. God had formerly spoken to His Old Testament people at the time of their constitution, when, from a mountain burning with fire to the heart of heaven, He had thundered the Decalogue, the 10 commandments. That was, we are told, a *"word spoken through angels,"* and so it was not to be regarded lightly. Israel, alas, discovered to their cost that every disobedience received a just recompense. This showed that God's Word through these "sent ones" proved steadfast. In our case, the Sent One (Apostle) is Jesus, and chapter one of Hebrews argues that He is "by so much better than the angels." Jesus' supremacy is established by virtue of His unique Sonship relation to God the Father, the fact that angels are instructed to worship Him, the special way in which He is addressed as God by God, the fact that He is the Creator, and because He has been exalted in His victory to the highest place.

Now, since God's Word has been brought to us by Jesus, the Apostle of our confession, One who is demonstrably so much better than the angels, *"therefore"* (2:1) we really ought to pay even more attention to that Word, bearing in mind that that which had been spoken through angels had proved steadfast. Indeed, we must be more careful than Israel not to neglect our salvation. This is a warning that a people needs to hear. The letter to the Hebrews envisages a divinely gathered people on earth engaged in the collective service of God. Remembering how Israel had been saved out of Egypt by blood, passed through the "baptism" of their Red Sea experience and then pledged their obedience to God's Word while arranged around Mount Sinai, we judge that this appeal from the heart of God has in view the anti-type of Israel's Sinai experience.

Jesus is described as the Apostle of our "confession." The full force of this word could be expressed as "to speak the same thing as another", or "to agree with someone else." When, at Sinai, Moses, God's apostle to His people then, brought the Word to them, their confession on that occasion was: *"all that the LORD hath spoken will we do, and be obedient"* (Ex.24:7). If today we find ourselves in a church of God, among the people of God, keeping the Word of God brought to us by Jesus the Apostle, then we have made the same confession, or should have. The thing that legitimizes a claim to be the people of God is this "good confession," or agreement to keep, in its entirety, the Word of God as delivered by the Apostle, and now written down for us by the apostles and prophets in the New Testament of our Bibles.

Some people find that they cannot agree with certain things in the New Testament. They appropriate to themselves the liberty to be selective in their obedience. That sort of attitude has no place among the people of God. God has spoken, and the people of God are to "speak the same thing." Our confession means agreeing with God even, alas, if it means disagreeing with other dear children of God.

Should we get discouraged, like Israel, perhaps by smallness locally or by lack of results, let us not be found putting God to the test by questioning: *"Is the LORD among us, or not?"* May we rather take as a timely word the encouragement to refocus our eyes on the Apostle of our confession, even Jesus. If we find ourselves in danger of "coming short" or "shrinking back" or not holding fast our boldness, let us look to Jesus. He is worthy of our undivided attention, since He is proclaimed here to be greater than the prophets, the angels and Moses.

17

THE ONE IN WHOM ALL THINGS WILL BE SUMMED UP (KARL SMITH)

In the old days at school, children were sometimes asked to read a complicated news report or chapter of a history book and summarise it in a certain number of words. This would show they had really understood the essential meaning of what they had read. We know that it is possible to sum up the Old Testament law. Even though a third-century Rabbi, Simlai, counted 613 separate commandments, Paul could say: *"For this. Thou shalt not commit adultery, Thou shalt not kill, Thou shalt not steal, Thou shalt not covet, and if there be any other commandment, it is summed up in this word, namely, Thou shalt love thy neighbour as thyself"* (1).

I, however, have been set the impossible task of writing a chapter about a verse in the Bible that takes in the whole universe, and the infinity of heaven as well, in 1500 words! Yet there is someone who can sum up all these things. Christ is spoken of as the one:

"in whom we have our redemption through his blood, the forgive-ness of our trespasses, according to the riches of his grace, which he made to abound toward us in all wisdom and prudence, having

made known unto us the mystery of his will, according to his good pleasure which he purposed in him unto a dispensation of the fulness of the times, to sum up all things in Christ, the things in the heavens, and the things upon the earth ..." (2).

I have chosen to quote both of these Bible verses in the Revised version, because it faithfully chooses the same expression 'sum up' to translate the one Greek word used in both passages. The English Standard version has *"to unite all things in him, things in heaven and things on earth."* The Authorized version puts it that *"he might gather together in one all things in Christ."* These slightly less literal interpretations nevertheless give us a picture of what the phrase means in practice.

God has generously revealed to us the mystery of his will - not only our own individual eternal destiny, but what He has planned to do with the whole universe. In the Lord Jesus, He will harmonise earth with heaven. We pray, *"Your kingdom come, your will be done, on earth as it is in heaven"* (3), because now this world is pulling in a radically different direction from heaven. Our governments and cultures (from the highest art to the gutter press) are often utterly opposed to the will of God. There is a day coming when this will not be so.

Predicting the tribe from which the Lord Jesus was descended, Jacob said, *"The sceptre shall not depart from Judah, nor the ruler's staff from between his feet, until Shiloh come; and unto him shall the obedience of the peoples be"* (4). This 'Shiloh' we take to be an Old Testament title of the Lord Jesus, the Lion of Judah. Not only Israel's descendants, but all nations would be obedient to Him. Before this, Abraham saw a blessing to come from his prophesied descendant that would go wider than the chosen race who would come from his line: *and in you all the families of the earth shall be blessed* (5). One effect of this universal obedience is a peace never before known on earth. The beautiful scene in Isaiah shows that:

> "He shall judge between the nations, ...
> and they shall beat their swords into ploughshares,
> and their spears into pruning hooks;
> nation shall not lift up sword against nation,
> neither shall they learn war anymore" (6).

Not only will all people be united, but even the animal kingdom will live harmoniously with us: "The wolf shall dwell with the lamb, and the leopard shall lie down with the young goat, and the calf and the lion and the fattened calf together; and a little child shall lead them" (7). No longer alienated from us by the effects of the Fall, they will be subject to our dominion fully as they were before it. It should not surprise us that all created things should one day escape the law of competition and aggression that seems to dominate relationships between them now, nor that they should be summed up in Christ with us, for *"All things were made through him, and without him was not any thing made that was made"* (8). They are the product of one hand and were made to serve one purpose: to glorify God in Him. We notice, however, that things under the earth (9) are not mentioned in Ephesians 1. There is no question of the forces of evil being summed up in Christ.

We who are described as 'in Christ' are enjoying some of the benefits of being gathered into one in Him even now. We are gathered into His body, in intimate relationship with Him as our head and with each other as completely interdependent parts of that body (10). He has summed up Jew and Gentile together into an international body that depends upon Him for everything. We take all our spiritual satisfaction and sustenance from Him. We have a unity of the Spirit and strive towards a unity of the faith (11) and of the knowledge of the Son of God as we conform to the Lord's teaching. This unity and maturity is described as the measure of the stature of the fullness of Christ (12). What an amazing thing for us to aspire to!

The summing up spoken of in Ephesians 1, however, will only be fully realised at the fullness of time (13). Everything that grows has a time of fullness, when it is at its peak or ripeness. History, too, has its time of completion. This will be seen when the Lord Jesus returns to this earth to reign as king in Jerusalem. At the moment, God's purposes for Israel as a nation are suspended following their rejection of the Messiah. His purposes in the present are fixed on the church the body of Christ and the new holy nation, open to Jews and Gentiles together, which gives it visible expression. We know that when the church is taken up, however, God will take up His plans for Israel again. It will be the tribes of Israel who will repentantly realise that the Lord Jesus was their Messiah and will endure persecution for their loyalty to Him (14). Even then, however, the message of the Lamb will not be contained in Israel alone - nor will they want it to be this time. Through their preaching they will rejoice to see:

> *"a great multitude that no one could number, from every nation, from all tribes and peoples and languages, standing before the throne and before the Lamb, clothed in white robes, with palm branches in their hands, and crying out with a loud voice, "Salvation belongs to our God who sits on the throne, and to the Lamb"* (15).

Finally the Lord Jesus will return with those who belong to Him in the Christian age to reign, to rule the world with His base in Jerusalem. It will be an international rule, the result of Calvary, but rooted in Israel.

This is why Paul speaks of us as being like olive branches grafted into the vine of the nation of Israel: *"For if you were cut from what is by nature a wild olive tree, and grafted, contrary to nature, into a cultivated olive tree, how much more will these, the natural branches, be grafted back into their own olive tree"* (16).

At the return of Christ, the tree will be a seamless whole. Those Christians who have been faithful to Him will reign with Him comfortably alongside the nation of Israel, refined through their suffering during the tribulation. Abraham's physical descendants will sit at the table with those who are sons of Abraham by following his example of faith (17). God's plans for us and them will be summed up perfectly in Christ. Having been summed up in Christ, all things will be handed over together to God: *"When all things are subjected to him, then the Son himself will also be subjected to him who put all things in subjection under him, that God may be all in all"* (18).

In his humility, God the Son acknowledges that He Himself is included in the Godhead and hands all things over to His Father. This will be the character of the eternal heavenly reality. How privileged we are to be in Christ!

References: (1) Rom.13:9 RV (2) Eph.1:7-10 RV (3) Matt.6:10 (4) Gen.49:10 RV (5) Gen.12:3 (6) Is.2:4 (7) Is.11:6 (8) Jn.1:3 (9) see Phil.2:10 (10) Rom.12:5 (11) Eph.4:3 (12) Eph.4:13 (13) Eph.1:10 (14) Rev.7:4-8 (15) Rev.7:9-10 (16) Rom.11:24 (17) see Gal.3 (18) 1 Cor.15:28

Bible quotations from the ESV, unless stated otherwise.

18

THE KINSMAN-REDEEMER (JAMES MARTIN)

Our appreciation of the redemptive work of the Lord Jesus will be greatly enhanced by a study of the aspects of redemption that are revealed in the Old Testament Scriptures. This is not surprising, for the things written aforetime were written for our learning, and the embryo of many a precious truth, fully revealed in our Lord Jesus Christ, though not fully appreciated by us, finds its place in the Old Testament.

At the very basis of man's relationship with God lies the fact that God has come out to "redeem" men to Himself. Here man's knowledge of God has its true beginning. The Hebrew word used is "Ga'al," which, in its primary sense, means "to make a claim," "to vindicate, in the sense of claiming something that has been lost or forfeited." Variously described by another scholar, it means "to resume a claim or right which has lapsed."

In practice the person who could fulfil this responsibility had to be one near of kin. Leviticus 25:25,49. give the order of right of redemption. This responsibility referred not only to lands and possessions, but also

85

to the redemption of a poor brother who had sold himself into bondage (Lev.25:25,47). The law seems also to hold within it the right of pre-emption, or the first refusal before exposure for sale. The book of Ruth and Jeremiah 32 provide interesting examples of the working out of this law in Israel. From the story of Ruth we may gather that it was also part of the kinsman's responsibility to marry the "wife of the dead to raise up the name of the dead upon his inheritance" (Ruth 4:5). Thus the Ga'al was not only one with a right laid on him because of near kinship, but he became a redeemer, in our accepted meaning of the word, namely, "one who buys back." He had to be both willing AND able to redeem.

A further shade of meaning comes into the word where the Ga'al is described as the *"avenger of blood"* (Deut.19:6; Num.35:12). At this juncture in Israel's history instructions for the appointing of cities of refuge are given. Perhaps the same meaning may be discerned in the memorable words of Job (19.25), when he said, "I know that my Redeemer (RV margin – 'vindicator') liveth." Proverbs 23:11 also suggests the meaning of an "Advocate." Thus, there are many cases where in the use of this word the idea of a money payment by the next of kin falls into the background and the meaning is purely "to save." "to deliver," or "to plead one's cause."

The word is extensively used in the Old Testament to describe the LORD in His saving work and activities towards Israel. It is a profitable study to meditate upon the many references. We have space for only a few. The LORD redeems (as a Ga'al) from destruction (Ps.103.4); from deceit (Ps.72:14); from oppression and violence (Ps.72:14); from captivity (Ps.107:2); from death (Hos.13:14); from Egypt (Ex.6:6); and from all evil (Gen.48:16). In many passages Israel describes the LORD as "Israel's Redeemer." These truths concerning the kinsman's responsibilities in redemption, simply recorded in precept and example in the Old

Testament Scriptures, have a deeper and fuller significance when we see them fulfilled in our blessed Lord Jesus Christ.

Concerning ourselves, the words of Isaiah are true, *"Behold, for your iniquities were ye sold"* (Is.50:1); *"Ye were sold for nought; and ye shall be redeemed without money"* (Is.52:8). To this all history bears witness, and the divine records confirm it, that we were *"sold under sin"* (Rom.7:14), becoming the bondservants of sin. But we can most fervently repeat the words of the women who came to cheer Naomi, *"Blessed be the LORD, which hath not left thee this day without a near kinsman, and let his name be famous in Israel. And he shall be unto thee a restorer of life, and a nourisher of thine old age"* (Ruth 4:14,15). In sublime language John records the wondrous fact that *"the Word became flesh, and dwelt among us ... full of grace and truth"* (Jn.1:14).

"Since then the children are sharers in blood and flesh, He also Himself in like manner partook of the same; ... For verily not of angels doth He take hold, but He taketh hold of the seed of Abraham" (Heb.2:14-16), are precious words recorded concerning the coming into this scene of the Son of God. By His birth in Bethlehem, He became very Man, liable to sorrows and temptations that afflict men, but He, Himself, was without sin (Heb.4:15). He is a very near Kinsman, and He is not ashamed to call us "brethren," but declares, *"Behold, I and the children which God hath given Me"* (Heb.2:11). In Him, we learn that *"we have our redemption through His blood, the forgiveness of our trespasses, according to the riches of His grace"* (Eph.1:7; Col.1:18). He has delivered us out of the hand of the Adversary when we could not redeem ourselves. Moreover, He has been the "Avenger" of blood in bringing *"to nought him that had the power of death, that is the devil"* (Heb.2:14).

Further, a rich provision is made for us ... for *"if any man sin, we have an Advocate with the Father, Jesus Christ, the Righteous"* (1 Jn.2:1). The *"precious blood ... even the blood of Christ"* is the liberating factor from a vain manner of life ... a life of empty tradition (see 1 Pet.1:18,19). He *"gave Himself for us, that He might redeem us from all iniquity, and purify unto Himself a people for His own possession, zealous of good works"* (Tit.2:14). Surely we have much reason to rejoice in that *"He entered in once for all into the holy place, having obtained ETERNAL redemption"* (Heb.9:12). We are conscious of the fact, however, that in company with the whole creation, we, even we, who *"have the firstfruits of the Spirit ... groan within ourselves, waiting for ... the redemption of our body"* (Rom.8:22,23).

When that grand day dawns, and our blessed Redeemer comes to claim His purchased possession, He *"shall fashion anew the body of our humiliation, that it may be conformed to the body of His glory"* (Phil.3:21). The apostle Paul quotes David (in Rom.4:7) as saying, *"Blessed are they whose sins are covered."* This takes us back to those powerful words of Job 33.24: *"Deliver him from going down to the pit, I have found a ransom."* The Hebrew word *"ransom"* (used here) is derived from a verb meaning *"to cover,"* being associated with the material that covers, and carries us further back to the instruction concerning the Ark that Noah built which was covered with bitumen for the preservation of his family. This Ark had to be covered *"within and without with pitch."*

We would suggest here, in passing, that a reading of Psalm 49:7-9, as it is punctuated in the Revised Version, will give a fuller meaning to the truth expressed in verse 7, namely, *"none of them can by any means redeem (Hebrew 'padah' - release) his brother, nor give to God a ransom (a cover) for him: ... that he should still live always ... (for the redemption of their soul is costly, and must be let alone for ever)."* This calls for great rejoicing that our Lord Jesus Christ has obtained, by His death and resurrection, eternal redemption.

Twice in the Gospels, Matthew 20:28, and Mark 10:45, we read that *"the Son of Man came ... to give His life a ransom* (Greek: 'lidron') *for many."* Here the word *"ransom"* means a *"loosing"* by the payment of an equivalent price ... a redemptive price. The little word "for" (Greek – 'anti') may mean *"in exchange for," "as the equivalent of,"* or *"instead of."* For we are *"justified freely by His grace through the redemption that is in Christ Jesus: whom God set forth to be a propitiation ..."* (Rom.3:24,25). In 1 Timothy 2.6 we read of *"Christ Jesus, who gave Himself a Ransom* (Greek: 'antilutron' - a substitutionary ransom) *for all."* Here the preposition 'for' is the Greek 'huper', and may be translated "on behalf of." How rich and liberal is this precious substitutionary Ransom for it is a provision for all mankind, although only those who avail themselves of its worth by appropriating faith will be among "the many" (Matthew 20.28), who will benefit from it!

The story of redemption, which in our language means "to buy back," is partially told out in the specific words used by men who *"spake from God, being moved by the Holy Spirit"* (2 Pet.1:21). "Agorazo" is the Greek word used in 1 Corinthians 6:20, and 1 Corinthians 7.28, for the twice repeated phrase "ye were bought with a price." This word primarily means "to frequent the market-place" (Greek: 'agora'), hence "to do business there, to buy." By adding the prefix, ex or ek, meaning "out of," the above word is strengthened - exagorazo means the purchasing of a slave, and taking him out of the market-place, never more to allow him to be put up for sale, but to give him his liberty and his freedom.

Thus Paul, encouraging the backsliding Galatians, used the word in chapter 3:18, *"Christ redeemed us from the curse of the law,"* yea, *"God sent forth His own Son, born of a woman, born under the law, that He might redeem them which were under the law ..."* (Gal.4:5-7). "With freedom did Christ set us free" (Gal.5:1). A strengthened form of "lutron" (already mentioned), namely, "apolutrosis," meaning a rich and full releasing, is used in 1 Corinthians 1:30. Here we have a liberation and a redemption from this scene of earth, as in Romans 8:28, "the redemption of our body." Wherefore we would remind ourselves of Paul's words to the Ephesians, *"Grieve not the Holy Spirit of God, in whom ye were sealed unto the day of redemption" (Eph.4:30).*

"Redemption! oh, wonderful story
Glad message for you and for me;
That Jesus has purchased our pardon,
And paid all the debt on the tree."
(S.M. Sayford)

"My Redeemer! oh what beauties
In that lovely name appear!
None but Jesus in His glories
Shall the honoured title wear."
(Anon.)

About Hayes Press

Hayes Press (www.hayespress.org) is a registered charity in the United Kingdom, whose primary mission is to disseminate the Word of God, mainly through literature. It is one of the largest distributors of gospel tracts and leaflets in the United Kingdom, with over 100 titles and many thousands dispatched annually. In addition to paperbacks and eBooks, Hayes Press also publishes Golden Bells, a popular daily Bible reading calendar

If you would like to contact Hayes Press, there are a number of ways you can do so:

By mail: c/o The Barn, Flaxlands, Royal Wootton Bassett, Wiltshire, UK SN4 8DY

By phone: 01793 850598

By eMail: info@hayespress.org

via Facebook: www.facebook.com/hayespress.org

Also by Hayes Press

Collected Writings on the Cross of Christ

This book takes a detailed look at the significance and ramifications of the most important event in human history, including the words of Jesus on the cross, the curse of the cross, the importance of the shedding of blood and the cross being prophesied.

Boaz, Ruth's Bridegroom, Redeemer and Lord of the Harvest

A heart-warming study of the book of Ruth - a jewelled cameo woven into the fabric of Israel's chequered background. The account of Ruth's arrival on the pages of God's Word is an interweaving of His grace, His call and His purpose. So, during Israel's dull days, she is like a colourful butterfly emerging from a very drab chrysalis. There is no shallow end to the story of Ruth, as depths of despair at the beginning lead on to deepening delight.

The Call of Christ

Be motivated to explore again the character of radical discipleship as opposed to pew-filling, sermon-tasting comfortable 'churchianity' which can end up as a sort of passive spectator sport. "The Call of Christ" is what being a disciple of Jesus is really all about: · Called to serve · Called to suffer · Called to die · Called to simple dependence on God · Called to be saints · Called as we are · Called to community · Called to obey · Called to possess God's hope · Called to share a heavenly calling. Each of the 12 modules in this course contain questions for further study.

9 798223 644651